# 3rd Edition
# Ventures 2
## WORKBOOK

**Gretchen Bitterlin** ▪ **Dennis Johnson** ▪ **Donna Price** ▪ **Sylvia Ramirez**
**K. Lynn Savage (Series Editor)**

**CAMBRIDGE**
UNIVERSITY PRESS

# CAMBRIDGE
## UNIVERSITY PRESS

University Printing House, Cambridge CB2 8BS, United Kingdom

One Liberty Plaza, 20th Floor, New York, NY 10006, USA

477 Williamstown Road, Port Melbourne, VIC 3207, Australia

314–321, 3rd Floor, Plot 3, Splendor Forum, Jasola District Centre, New Delhi – 110025, India

79 Anson Road, #06–04/06, Singapore 079906

Cambridge University Press is part of the University of Cambridge.

It furthers the University's mission by disseminating knowledge in the pursuit of education, learning and research at the highest international levels of excellence.

www.cambridge.org
Information on this title: www.cambridge.org/9781108450003

© Cambridge University Press 2018

First published 2008
Second edition 2014

20  19  18  17  16  15  14  13  12  11

Printed in Dubai by Oriental Press

*A catalogue record for this publication is available from the British Library*

ISBN  978-1-108-44956-4  Student's Book
ISBN  978-1-108-44941-0  Online Workbook
ISBN  978-1-108-66609-1  Teacher's Edition
ISBN  978-1-108-44921-2  Class Audio CDs
ISBN  978-1-108-44912-0  Presentation Plus

Additional resources for this publication at www.cambridge.org/ventures

# CONTENTS

# WELCOME

## 1 Meet your classmates

**A** What are the people doing? Complete the sentences. Use the words in the box.

> help   read   speak   use   write

1. Bao _is reading_ a book.

2. Claudia _is using_ a computer.

3. Sara _is speaking_ on the phone.

4. Ana and Amy _are writing_ on the board.

5. Wei _is helping_ Raul with his homework.

**B** Complete the answers.

1. **A** Is Claudia reading?

   **B** _No_, _she isn't_.

2. **A** Is Wei helping Raul with his homework?

   **B** _Yes_, _he is_.

3. **A** Is Sara sleeping?

   **B** _No_, _she isn't_.

4. **A** Are Ana and Amy reading?

   **B** _No_, _they aren't_.

5. **A** Is Claudia using a computer?

   **B** _Yes_, _she is_.

6. **A** Is Bao reading a book?

   **B** _Yes_, _he is_.

## 2 Skills

**A** Read the sentences. Look at the chart. Circle T (True) or F (False). Then correct the false statements.

| Skill | Ivan | Irma | Oscar | Lara | Joe | Sandy |
|---|---|---|---|---|---|---|
| speak Spanish | | ✓ | | | | |
| speak Chinese | | | | | | ✓ |
| cook | | | ✓ | | | |
| iron | | | | | ✓ | |
| swim | | | | ✓ | | |
| use a computer | ✓ | ✓ | | | | |
| drive a truck | | ✓ | | | | ✓ |

1. Ivan can cook.                          T   (F)   _Ivan can't cook._

2. Lara can't speak Spanish.               (T)  F    _____

3. Ivan and Irma can speak Chinese.        T   (F)   _Ivan and Irma can't speak Chinese_

4. Irma can't iron.                        (T)  F    _____

5. Joe can swim.                           T   (F)   _Joe can't swim._

6. Sandy can drive a truck.                (T)  F    _____

7. Oscar and Lara can use a computer.      T   (F)   _Oscar and Lara can't use a computer._

8. Irma can't drive a truck.               T   (F)   _Irma can drive a truck._

**B** Listen to the conversation. Check Lisa's skills.

_✓_ speak English        _✓_ write Chinese

_✓_ speak Chinese        ___ use computers

___ drive a truck        _✓_ cook

I'm looking for a job. - ESTOU a procura de um emprego
I'm going to lear - vou aprender

## ③ Verb tense review (present and past of *be* verb)

**A** Complete the story. Use *am*, *is*, *are*, *was*, *were*, and *weren't*.

My name ___is___ Rafael. I ___am___ from
  1.                          2.
El Salvador. My wife's name ___is___ Celia. She
                             3.
___is___ from El Salvador, too. There ___are___
  4.                                        5.
two children in our family – one son and one

daughter. Our son, Tomás, ___is___ 13 years old.
                            6.
Our daughter, Claudia, ___is___ 14 years old.
                         7.
Tomás and Claudia ___were___ born in the U.S. Celia and I ___were___ born in the U.S. We
                    8.                                       9.
___were___ born in El Salvador.
  10.

Tomás and Claudia ___are___ students. They ___are___ both very smart!
                    11.                       12.
I ___am___ a teacher in El Savador, but now I ___was___ a cook. Celia ___was___ a
  13.                                          14.                    15.
nurse in El Salvador, but now she ___is___ a student, just like Tomás and Claudia.
                                   16.
We ___are___ all very busy, but we ___are___ very happy.
    17.                              18.

**B** Read the chart. Complete the sentences.

| | What is your name? | Where are you from? | What was your occupation there? | Are you married? | How many people are in your family? |
|---|---|---|---|---|---|
| 1. | Diego | Mexico | truck driver | Yes | five |
| 2. | Bae | Korea | student | No | two |

1. My name ___is Diego___ . ___I am___ from Mexico.
   I ___was a truck driver___ in Mexico. I ___am___
   married. ___There are five___ people in my family.

2. My name ___is Bae___ . ___I am___ from Korea.
   I ___was student___ in Korea. I ___'m not___
   married. ___There are two___ people in my family.

## 4 Verb tense review (present and past of regular and irregular verbs)

**A** Read Henry's journal. Write the correct verb.

We did a lot last weekend! I usually _____work_____ every Saturday, but last Saturday,
1. work / worked

I _____went_____ to a ball game. Sarah usually _____goes_____ shopping on Saturday, but she
2. go / went          3. goes / went

_____came_____ to the game with me. We _____had_____ a lot of fun last Saturday!
4. come / came          5. have / had

Last Sunday, I _____went_____ to work. I _____worked_____ last Sunday because
6. go / went          7. work / worked

I _____didn't go_____ to work on Saturday. I usually _____take_____ the bus to work, but last
8. don't go / didn't go          9. take / took

Sunday, I _____slept_____ late. I _____didn't take_____ the bus, so I _____walked_____
10. sleep / slept          11. didn't take / don't take          12. walk / walked

to work!

We _____visit_____ my parents every weekend, too. We _____go_____ to their house
13. visit / visited          14. go / went

for dinner every Sunday night. But last Sunday, we _____went_____ to a restaurant for
15. go / went

dinner. We _____celebrated_____ my parents' anniversary last Sunday night. On
16. celebrate / celebrated

Monday morning, I was really tired!

**B** Fill in the missing words. Use the correct tense.

1. Andy _____slept_____ late yesterday.
       (sleep)
2. Mari usually _____works_____ on the weekend.
                (work)
3. Bill _____takes_____ the bus to school every day.
         (take)
4. We _____visited_____ our grandparents last week.
         (visit)
5. Anna _____walked_____ to school yesterday.
          (walk)
6. Sachi _____went_____ to a ball game last Saturday.
          (go)
7. Jack usually _____celebrates_____ his birthday at a restaurant.
                 (celebrate)
8. She _____doesn't_____ _____buy_____ anything at the mall yesterday.
       (not)          (buy)

Check your answers. See page 132.

# UNIT 1 PERSONAL INFORMATION

## Lesson A Listening

**1** **Look at the picture. Write the words.**

curly hair     long brown hair     short blond hair     striped pants
a jogging suit     a long skirt     short brown hair     a white T-shirt

Alejandro

1. _curly hair_

2. _Short brown hair_

3. _a joggin suit_

4. _striped pants_

Carlos

5. _short blond hair_

Jane

6. _long brown hair_

7. _white T shirt_

8. _a long skirt_

Sandra

**2** **Complete the sentences. Use the words from Exercise 1.**

1. Alejandro has _curly hair_.

2. Alejandro is wearing _striped pants_.

3. Jane has _short blond hair_.

4. Jane is wearing _white T-shirt_.

5. Carlos has _short brown hair_.

6. Carlos is wearing _a joggin suit_.

7. Sandra has _long brown hair_.

8. Sandra is wearing _a long skirt_.

_blond = light brown hair_

**Write the words.**

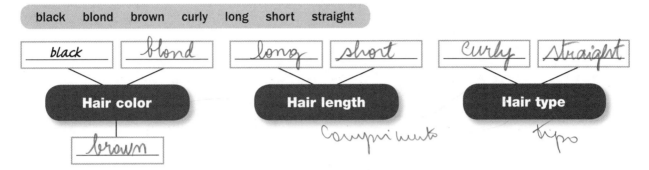

| black | blond | brown | curly | long | short | straight |

| black | *blond* | | *long* | *short* | | *curly* | *straight* |

**Hair color**

**Hair length**       *Compliments*

**Hair type**       *typo*

*brown*

 **Listen. Circle the correct answers.**

**Conversation A**

1. James is wearing _____.
   a. extra large pants
   b. a jogging suit *(circled)*
   c. a soccer uniform

2. James has _____.
   a. short curly hair *(circled)*
   b. long hair
   c. short blond hair

**Conversation B**

3. Lisa is _____.
   a. Miles's wife *(circled)*
   b. James's wife
   c. Miles's daughter

4. Lisa has _____.
   a. long blond hair
   b. short dark hair
   c. short blond hair *(circled)*

**Conversation C**

5. Sara is _____.
   a. pretty *(circled)*
   b. athletic
   c. tall

6. Sara looks like _____.
   a. Miles
   b. James
   c. Lisa *(circled)*

Study the chart on page 131.

**1** **Write the words in the correct order.**

1. striped / a / green and white / dress
   *a green and white striped dress*

2. shirt / checked / black and blue / a
   *a black and blue checked shirt*

3. a / blue / coat / long
   *a long blue coat*

4. small / shoes / white and black
   *small white and black shoes.*

5. pants / black / plaid
   *black plaid pants*

6. boots / brown / short
   *short brown boots*

**2** **Look at the pictures. Write the words from Exercise 1.**

1. _a long blue coat_

2. _small white and black shoes_

3. _____

4. _black plaid pants_

5. _a black and blue checked shirt_

6. _a green and white striped dress_

**3** **Read the sentences. Look at the ad. Circle the correct answers.**

1. Model A is wearing a _____ skirt.
   a. plaid
   b. striped
   c. checked

2. Model A has _____ hair.
   a. long curly   *eucaracolado comprido*
   b. short straight   *curto liso*
   c. long straight   *longo liso*

3. Model B has _____ hair.
   a. long curly
   b. short curly
   c. short straight

4. Model C is wearing a _____ shirt.
   a. plaid
   b. striped
   c. checked

5. Model D is wearing a striped _____.
   a. sweater
   b. pants
   c. skirt

6. Model E is wearing a long _____.
   a. sweater
   b. coat
   c. dress

**4** **Write the words.**

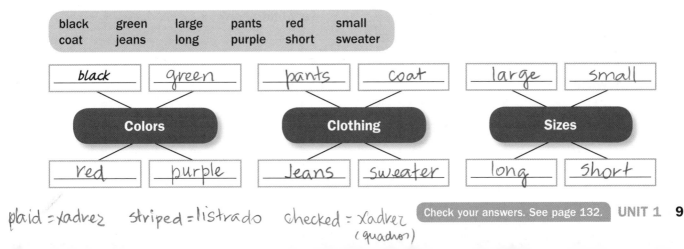

| black | green | large | pants | red | small |
| coat | jeans | long | purple | short | sweater |

Colors: black, green, red, purple

Clothing: pants, coat, jeans, sweater

Sizes: large, small, long, short

*plaid = xadrez   striped = listrado   checked = xadrez (quadros)*

# Lesson C  What are you doing right now?

Study the chart on page 126.

## 1  Read the questions. Circle the answers.

1. What are you doing right now?
   a. I study for a test.
   b.) I'm studying for a test.

2. What do you usually do at night?
   a.) I usually study English.
   b. I am usually studying English.

3. What do you always wear to work?
   a. I'm always wearing my uniform.
   b.) I always wear my uniform.

4. What are you wearing today?
   a.) I'm wearing jeans and a shirt.
   b. I wear jeans and a shirt.

5. What do you usually do on the weekend?
   a.) I visit with my family.
   b. I'm visiting with my family.

6. What do you do every Tuesday?
   a. I'm going to the park.
   b.) I go to the park.

## 2  Complete the conversations. Use the correct form of the verb. Use *am, is, are, do,* or *does.*

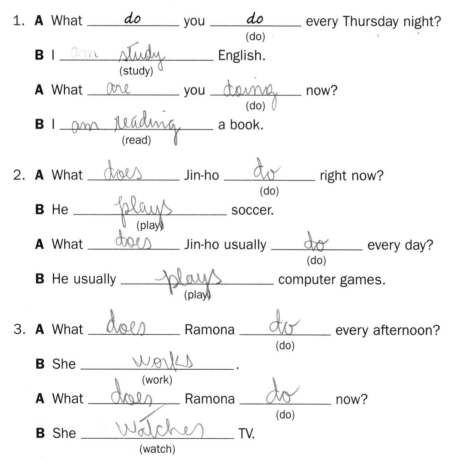

1. **A** What _____do_____ you _____do_____ every Thursday night?
   (do)

   **B** I _____am study_____ English.
   (study)

   **A** What _____are_____ you _____doing_____ now?
   (do)

   **B** I _____am reading_____ a book.
   (read)

2. **A** What _____does_____ Jin-ho _____do_____ right now?
   (do)

   **B** He _____plays_____ soccer.
   (play)

   **A** What _____does_____ Jin-ho usually _____do_____ every day?
   (do)

   **B** He usually _____plays_____ computer games.
   (play)

3. **A** What _____does_____ Ramona _____do_____ every afternoon?
   (do)

   **B** She _____works_____ .
   (work)

   **A** What _____does_____ Ramona _____do_____ now?
   (do)

   **B** She _____watches_____ TV.
   (watch)

Letter S — SOUND sss

## ❸ Circle the correct question.

1. He goes home.
   a. What does he do at 9:00? *(circled)*
   b. What is he doing right now?

2. He calls the office.
   a. What does he do every Monday? *(circled)*
   b. What is he doing now?

3. He's watching a movie.
   a. What does he do every night?
   b. What is he doing right now? *(circled)*

4. He's drinking orange juice.
   a. What does he drink every day?
   b. What is he drinking now? *(circled)*

5. He sits at his desk.
   a. Where does he sit every night? *(circled)*
   b. Where is he sitting right now?

6. He's wearing a striped suit.
   a. What does he wear to work every day?
   b. What is he wearing today? *(circled)*

## ❹ Complete the sentences. Use the simple present form of the verbs. Then listen.

call   go   leave   sit   study   talk

Eduardo usually __leaves__ English class at 9:00 p.m. He __goes__ home and __calls__ his girlfriend, Lisa. They usually __talk__ for 15 minutes. Then Eduardo __sits__ at his desk. He __studies__ English late at night.

## ❺ Complete the sentences. Use the present continuous form of the verbs. Then listen.

drink   relax   sit   speak   watch   wear

Tonight, Eduardo __is relaxing__. He __is watching__ TV with Lisa. They __are sitting__ on the sofa. He __is drinking__ a soda. He __is wearing__ jeans and a shirt. He __is speaking__ English with Lisa. She is a good teacher!

# Lesson D  Reading

**1** **Read and complete the chart with the underlined words in the email. Then listen.**

---

From: | Mira Hernandez
To: | Julia Yee
Date: | January 2, 2018 2:06 p.m.
Subject: | How are you?

Dear Julia,

I <u>think</u> about you every day. I'm at work right now. I <u>am writing</u> this email in the lunchroom. We <u>miss</u> you here. How is Chicago? We <u>are working</u> very hard. New York <u>is</u> very cold right now. Today I <u>am wearing</u> my jacket, hat, and scarf! The kids both <u>go</u> to school every day. Gabriel <u>wears</u> a uniform to school. It's very cute. Mica <u>goes</u> to a different school. She wears jeans every day.
Please write back!

Lots of love,
Mira

---

| Present continuous | *am writing* | | are working | am wearing |
|---|---|---|---|---|
| Simple present | *think* | miss | is    go | wears    goes |

**2** **Answer the questions. Use the information from Exercise 1.**

1. Where is Mira right now?
   *She's in the lunchroom.*

2. What city does Julia live in?
   *Julia lives in Chicago - State Illinois*

3. What city does Mira live in?
   *She lives in New York*

4. What does Gabriel wear to school?
   *Gabriel wears a uniform*

5. What does Mica wear to school every day?
   *She wears jeans*

6. What is Mira doing right now?
   *She is working*

## 3 Find the words.

| belt | earrings | hat | purse | scarf | tie |
| bracelet | gloves | necklace | ring | sunglasses | watch |

column – kälam
line – linhs

|    | 1 | 2 | 3 | 4 | 5 | 6 | 7 | 8 | 9 | 10 | 11 | 12 |
|----|---|---|---|---|---|---|---|---|---|----|----|----|
| 1  | t | f | d | b | a | w | t | o | m | d | e | a |
| 2  | e | t | g | l | o | v | e | s | d | n | a | v |
| 3  | t | n | p | c | b | e | x | u | a | p | r | p |
| 4  | i | z | z | h | a | t | a | n | c | l | r | w |
| 5  | a | n | y | r | d | o | b | g | v | m | i | a |
| 6  | n | t | d | g | m | b | e | l | p | b | n | t |
| 7  | a | p | u | r | s | e | l | a | e | h | g | c |
| 8  | x | v | r | s | k | f | t | s | s | t | s | h |
| 9  | d | v | i | n | t | i | e | s | c | a | r | f |
| 10 | h | b | n | b | r | a | c | e | l | e | t | p |
| 11 | r | a | g | i | k | j | j | s | q | w | w | c |
| 12 | t | n | e | c | k | l | a | c | e | d | d | i |

## 4 Look at the picture. Write the words from Exercise 3.

1. _earrings_
2. a scarf
3. a necklace
4. a belt
5. a bracelet
6. a ring
7. a purse
8. a hat
9. sunglasses
10. a Tie
11. a watch
12. gloves

# Lesson E Writing

Study the chart on page 131.

## 1 Read the chart. Complete the paragraphs.

|  | Sarah | Martina | Norma |
|---|---|---|---|
| Hair color | brown | blond | black |
| Eye color | brown | blue | green |
| Clothes | red and white striped sweater, blue jeans | black shirt, black pants, red shoes | blue jacket, yellow shirt, gray plaid skirt |
| Accessories | scarf, hat | gold watch, red purse | large earrings, rings |
| After-class activities | go to work | go out with friends | go home |
| Weekend activities | exercise, play with children | study English, clean house | visit with family, watch children play sports |

**A**

This person has black hair and ___green___ eyes. She ___goes___ home
1.                                               2.
every day after class. On the weekend, she ___visits___ with her family and
3.
___watches___ her children play sports. She is wearing a blue ___jacket___,
4.                                                                5.
large ___earrings___, and rings. Who is she? ___She is Norma___
6.                                              7.

**B**

This person has ___brown___ eyes and brown hair. She's wearing a red and
1.
___white___ striped sweater and blue ___jeans___. She ___goes___ to
2.                                        3.                    4.
work after class every day. On the weekend, she exercises and ___plays___
5.
with her children. Who is she? ___She's Sarah___
6.

**C**

Today, this person is ___wearing___ black clothing. Her ___shoes___ and purse
1.                                                       2.
are red. She has ___blond___ hair and ___blue___ eyes. After class, she
3.                            4.
___goes___ out with her friends. On the weekend, she ___studies___ English
5.                                                    6.
and cleans her house. Who is this person? ___She's Martina___
7.

**2** **Rewrite the sentences. Change the underlined words. Use the words below.**

√ a backpack  √ every Monday  √ is wearing
√ a watch  √ is long  √ on the weekend

1. Bobby goes to New York City every Saturday and Sunday.

   *Bobby goes to New York City on the weekend.*

2. Georgia is in a black scarf and a red coat.

   *Georgia is wearing a black scarf and a red coat*

3. Susana goes to work after school on Monday.

   *Susana goes to work after school every Monday*

4. Mei's hair isn't short.

   *Mei's hair is long*

5. Martin is carrying his books in a bag on his back.

   *Martin is carrying his books in a backpack*

6. Christina is wearing a bracelet with a small clock on it.

   *Christina is wearing a watch*

**3** **Rewrite the sentences in a different way.**

1. Mary teaches English on the weekend.

   *On the weekend, Mary teaches English.*

2. Every night, Sam leaves early.

   *Sam leaves early every night*

3. On Thursday, Alberto watches TV.

   *Alberto watches TV on Thursdays*

4. Raquel plays soccer on Saturday.

   *On Saturday, Raquel plays soccer.*

5. Michael wears a suit every Sunday.

   *Every sunday, Michael wears a suit,*

6. Every June, Petra has a birthday party.

   *Petra has a birthday party every June.*

# Lesson F Another view

**1** **Read the questions. Look at the ad. Fill in the correct answers.**

**ALLENE'S ATTIC ONE-DAY SALE**

**TODAY ONLY! OPEN 7:00 A.M.-MIDNIGHT!**

$14.00

$19.99

$22.00

$95.00

$100.00

$120.00

$62.00

$9.50

$12.00

$25.00

$45.00

$46.50

1. How much does the plaid shirt cost?
   - (A) $14.00
   - (B) $22.00
   - ● $25.00
   - (D) $32.00

2. Which item costs $12.00?
   - (A) the necklace
   - (B) the ring
   - ● the scarf
   - (D) the tie

3. When does Allene's Attic close today?
   - (A) 7:00 a.m.
   - (B) 10:00 a.m.
   - (C) noon
   - ● midnight

4. Which item costs $62.00?
   - ● the purse
   - (B) the boots
   - (C) the coat
   - (D) the necklace

5. How much do the pants cost? *Calça*
   - (A) $20.00
   - (B) $32.00
   - ● $45.00
   - (D) $100.00

6. Which statement is true?
   - (A) The earrings cost more than the necklace.
   - (B) The scarf costs more than the tie.
   - (C) The skirt *saia* costs more than the pants.
   - ● All of the above.

**2** **Look at the chart. Complete the sentences.**

| | Rachel | Rob | Dan | Alicia | Luke |
|---|---|---|---|---|---|
| Do you wear glasses? | ✓ | | ✓ | | |
| Do you like sports? | | ✓ | | ✓ | |
| Do you have a job? | ✓ | ✓ | | | ✓ |
| Do you usually eat breakfast? | | ✓ | ✓ | | |
| Do you watch TV every night? | ✓ | | ✓ | | ✓ |
| Do you wear a scarf? | | | | ✓ | |
| Do you wear a hat? | ✓ | | | | |
| Do you usually wear a watch? | | ✓ | | ✓ | ✓ |

1. Rachel wears glasses, _and Dan does, too_.
(Dan)

2. Luke doesn't wear a hat, _and Rob doesn't, too_.
(Rob)

3. Alicia likes sports, _and Rachel doesn't_.
(Rachel)

4. Luke has a job, _and Rob does too_.
(Rob)

5. Rob doesn't wear a scarf, _and Luke doesn't, too_.
(Luke)

6. Dan usually eats breakfast, _and Alicia doesn't_.
(Alicia)

7. Alicia wears a watch, _and Luke does, too_.
(Luke)

8. Rob doesn't watch TV every night, _and Alicia doesn't, too_.
(Alicia)

9. Alicia likes sports, _and Dan doesn't_.
(Dan)

10. Dan doesn't wear a watch, _and Rachel doesn't, too_.
(Rachel)

# UNIT 2 AT SCHOOL

## Lesson A Listening

**1** **Write the words.**

| a computer lab | a hall | a keyboard | a lab instructor | a monitor | a mouse | a student |

1.   *a computer lab*

4. _____

5. _____

2. _____

6. _____

7. _____

3. _____

**2** **Complete the conversation.**

| computer | instructor | keyboarding | register | skill | work |

1. **A** Hi. I need to learn _____*keyboarding*_____.
   1.

   **B** Great. I'm Ms. Moreno. I'm the _____instructor_____. Why do you
   2.

   want to learn to use a _____computer_____?
   3.

2. **A** I need to learn for my _____work_____.
   4.

   **B** That's great. Keyboarding is an important _____skill_____. Did you
   5.

   _____register_____ in the office?
   6.

3. **A** Yes.

   **B** OK. Have a seat, please.

## 3 Read Diego's schedule. Answer the questions.

Name: *Diego Sanchez*
Student ID: *555-23-0967*

| Class | Room | Day | Time | Teacher |
|-------|------|-----|------|---------|
| English | H102 | MW | 6:00–7:50 p.m. | Hilary Bowman |
| Computer lab | H315 | MW | 8:00–9:50 p.m. | Jane Moreno |

1. Who is Ms. Bowman?                          *Diego's English instructor*
2. Who is Ms. Moreno?                           *Diego's Computer lab instructor*
3. What is Diego's student ID number?   *555-23-0967*
4. Where is the English class?               *Room H102*
5. When is the English class?               *MW*
6. What class is in room H315?             *Computer lab*

## 4 Listen. Circle T (True) or F (False).

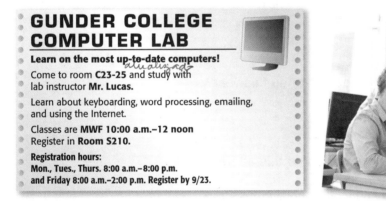

**GUNDER COLLEGE COMPUTER LAB**

**Learn on the most up-to-date computers!**

Come to room **C23-25** and study with lab instructor **Mr. Lucas**.

Learn about keyboarding, word processing, emailing, and using the Internet.

Classes are **MWF 10:00 a.m.–12 noon** Register in **Room S210**.

**Registration hours:**
Mon., Tues., Thurs. 8:00 a.m.–8:00 p.m.
and Friday 8:00 a.m.–2:00 p.m. Register by 9/23.

**Conversation A**

1. Malik and Jenn are in a computer class.          T   (F)
2. Malik wants to register for a computer class.    (T)  F
3. Ms. Grant helped Jenn find an English class.     T   (F)

**Conversation B**

4. Malik needs to learn computers for his job.      T   (F)
5. Ms. Grant is the computer lab instructor.        T   (F)
6. The computer lab is near the library.            (T)  F

**Conversation C**

7. Malik doesn't want to learn keyboarding.         (T)  F
8. Computer classes are in the morning.             T   F
9. Malik will come to class on Thursday.            T   (F)

*up to date = atualizado*

Check your answers. See page 133. **UNIT 2** **19**

# Lesson B  What do you want to do?

Study the chart on page 127.

## 1  Match the wants and needs.

1. Lynn wants to fix cars. __f__
2. Joe wants to finish high school. __e__
3. I want to get a driver's license. __d__
4. Li and Matt want to become citizens. __b__
5. Ann wants to make more money. __c__
6. Karl wants to learn keyboarding. __a__

a. He needs to take a computer class.
b. They need to take a citizenship class.
c. She needs to get a second job.
d. I need to take driving lessons.
e. He needs to take a GED class.
f. She needs to study auto mechanics.

## 2  Complete the sentences.

1. **A** What _____does_____ Maria need to do to get a driver's license?
   (do / does)

   **B** She _____needs to take_____ driving lessons.
   (need / take)

2. **A** What _____does_____ Jim want to do next year?
   (do / does)

   **B** He _____wants to go_____ to community college.
   (want / go)

3. **A** What _____does_____ Carrie want to do this year?
   (do / does)

   **B** She _____wants to get_____ a second job.
   (want / get)

4. **A** What _____do_____ you want to do this afternoon?
   (do / does)

   **B** I _____want to talk_____ to a counselor about the GED.
   (want / talk)

5. **A** Excuse me. _____Do_____ you need help?
   (Do / Does)

   **B** Yes, thanks. I _____need to learn_____ keyboarding skills.
   (need / learn)

6. **A** _____Do_____ you need any assistance?
   (Do / Does)

   **B** Yes, thank you. I _____need to register_____ for a citizenship class.
   (need / register)

**3** **Read the catalog and answer the questions. Then listen.**

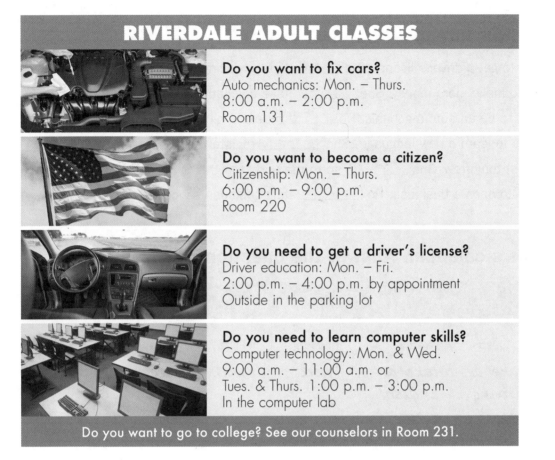

**RIVERDALE ADULT CLASSES**

**Do you want to fix cars?**
Auto mechanics: Mon. – Thurs.
8:00 a.m. – 2:00 p.m.
Room 131

**Do you want to become a citizen?**
Citizenship: Mon. – Thurs.
6:00 p.m. – 9:00 p.m.
Room 220

**Do you need to get a driver's license?**
Driver education: Mon. – Fri.
2:00 p.m. – 4:00 p.m. by appointment
Outside in the parking lot

**Do you need to learn computer skills?**
Computer technology: Mon. & Wed.
9:00 a.m. – 11:00 a.m. or
Tues. & Thurs. 1:00 p.m. – 3:00 p.m.
In the computer lab

Do you want to go to college? See our counselors in Room 231.

1. **A** Carlos wants to fix cars. What class does he need to take?

   **B** *He needs to take an auto mechanics class.*

2. **A** My mother needs to get a driver's license. What class does she need to take?

   **B** She needs to take a driver education class.

3. **A** My wife and I want to become citizens. What class do we need to take?

   **B** You need to take citizenship class.

4. **A** Arthur is taking an auto mechanics class. What room does he need to go to?

   **B** He needs to go to Room 131.

5. **A** You want to go to college. What room do you need to go to?

   **B** I need to go to Room 231.

6. **A** My sisters want to learn computer skills. What class do they need to take?

   **B** They need to take computer technology class.

## Lesson C  What will you do?

Study the chart on page 129.

**1  Complete the sentences. Use *will* or *won't*.**

1. Javier needs to get a driver's license. He ___will___ take driving lessons next month.
2. Sally wants to make more money. She _will_ take a vocational course.
3. Abram wants to be an auto mechanic. He _Won't_ take a citizenship class.
4. Amelia needs to learn a new language. She _will_ register for a class next week.
5. Min has a test tomorrow. She _Won't_ go to the party tonight.
6. Micah needs to open a business. He _will_ start business school soon.

**2  Read James's calendar. Answer the questions.**

| JAMES'S CALENDAR | | | | | | |
|---|---|---|---|---|---|---|
| Monday | Tuesday | Wednesday | Thursday | Friday | Saturday | Sunday |
| take an English class | take a driving lesson | take an English class | work | work | meet Lisa for lunch | call Mom |

1. What will James do on Thursday?
   _He'll work on Thursday._

2. What will he do on Tuesday?
   _He'll take a driving lesson_

3. What will he do on Friday?
   _He'll work on Friday_

4. What will he do on Saturday?
   _He'll call his Mom_

5. What will he do on Sunday?
   _He'll meet Lisa for lunch_

6. What will he do on Monday and Wednesday?
   _He'll will take an English class_

**3** **Look at the pictures. Complete the sentences.**

Suk-jin's Plan

This year: go to the U.S.

Next year: study English

In two years: get a GED

In three years: take a vocational course

In four years: open a business

In five years: buy a house

1. **A** What will Suk-jin do in five years?

   **B** He'll probably _buy a house_ .

2. **A** What will he do this year?

   **B** Maybe he'll _go To the U.S._ .

3. **A** What will he do in four years?

   **B** He'll probably _Open a business_ .

4. **A** What will he do next year?

   **B** Maybe he'll _study English_ .

5. **A** What will he do in two years?

   **B** Most likely he'll _get a GED_ .

6. **A** What will he do in three years?

   **B** He'll probably _take a vocational course_ .

**4** **Write questions.**

1. What / she / in five years _What will she do in five years?_
2. What / he / next year _what will he do next year?_
3. What / you / tomorrow _What will you do tomorrow_
4. What / they / this weekend _what will they this weekend?_

# Lesson D Reading

**1** **Read and answer the questions about the ad. Then listen.**

## Learn Computer Technology at City College

Get a job as a computer technician in 18 months! No time? Don't worry. All courses are at night and on weekends.

*There will be an information session on March 14 at 7:30 at City College.*

We'll talk about registration, the classes, and the certificate. Come and ask questions! Teachers and current students will be there.

1. How long is the Computer Technology program? __18 months.__
2. When is the information session? __March 14 at 7:30__
3. Where is the information session? __At City College__
4. What will they discuss at the information session? __They will talk about registration, the classes, and the certificate.__
5. Who will be there from the school? _____

**2** **Read about Megan's goal. Circle the correct answers.**

### My Goal

I want to open my own coffee shop. I need to take three steps. *etapas* First, I need to take business classes. Second, I need to get a job in a coffee shop. Third, I need to learn about the coffee-shop business. I think I can reach my goal in three years.

1. Megan wants to _____.
   a. become a citizen
   (b.) open a coffee shop
   c. finish high school

2. First, she needs to _____.
   a. get her GED
   b. get a job
   (c.) take business classes

3. Second, she needs to _____.
   a. learn about the coffee-shop business
   b. open her coffee shop
   (c.) get a job in a coffee shop

4. In three years, Megan will probably _____.
   (a.) open her coffee shop
   b. get a job in a dress shop
   c. finish business school

**3** **Match the names of the vocational courses.**

1. computer __e__
2. criminal __d__
3. fitness __a__
4. home health __b__
5. small engine __c__

√a. training
√b. care
√c. repair
√d. justice
√e. networking

**4** **Look at the pictures. Write the vocational courses.**

√computer networking  √criminal justice  √fitness training  √hotel management
√counseling  √dental assisting  √home health care  √small engine repair

## Study at Peterson Vocational School!

We offer:

1. _computer networking_

2. _dental assisting_

3. _fitness training_

4. _criminal Justice_

5. _small engine repair_

6. _hotel management_

7. _home health care_

8. _counseling_

# Lesson E  Writing

##  1  Match the goals with the steps.

**Goals**

1. Pablo wants to finish high school. __b__
2. Elena wants to learn keyboarding. __d__
3. Jeff wants to learn how to fix cars. __f__
4. They want to study criminal justice. __a__
5. Marina wants to become a citizen. __c__
6. Toan wants to speak and understand English. __e__

**Steps needed to reach the goals** *alcanzar os objetivos*

✓a. They need to take criminal justice classes. *General Educating High School*

✓b. He needs to take the GED test.

✓c. She needs to take a citizenship class.

✓d. She needs to take a computer class.

✓e. He needs to make English-speaking friends.

✓f. He needs to take an automotive repair class.

## 2  Read and complete the sentences. Then listen.

### My Goal for Next Year

I have a new goal for next year. I want to get a second job on the weekend. I need to make more money because we have a new baby. I will take three steps to reach my goal. First, I need to talk to people about job possibilities. Second, I need to look for jobs in the newspaper. Third, I need to look for jobs online. I will probably reach my goal in two months.

1. Quan wants to _get a second job on the weekend._
2. He needs more money because _he has a new baby._
3. First, he needs to _talk to people about job possibilities._
4. Second, he needs to _look for jobs in the newspaper._
5. Third, he needs to _look for jobs online._
6. He will probably reach his goal in _two months._

## 3 Complete the sentences.

children   First   goal   Second   Third   year

# Rachel's Goal

Rachel has a big ___goal___. She wants
                    1.
to help her ___children___ with their homework.
                    2.
___First___, she needs to find an adult school.
     3
___Second___, she needs to practice her English
          4.
every day. ___Third___, she needs to volunteer
                    5.
with the Parent-Teacher Association (PTA) at her
children's school. She'll probably be ready to help
her children next ___year___.
                    6.

## 4 Answer the questions. Use the story in Exercise 3.

1. What is Rachel's goal?
   _She wants to help her children with their homework._

2. What does Rachel need to do first?
   _She needs to find an adult school._

3. What does Rachel need to do second?
   _She needs to practice her English every day._

4. What does Rachel need to do third?
   _She needs to volunteer with the Parent-Teacher Association (PTA) at her children's school._

5. When will Rachel be ready to help her children?
   _She'll probably be ready to help her children next year._

# Lesson F Another view

**1 Read the questions. Look at the college catalog. Fill in the correct answers.**

## ORANGE COUNTY COMMUNITY COLLEGE

| Catalog Page | Courses | Spring | Summer | Fall |
|---|---|---|---|---|
| 51 | Criminal Justice | 📖 | | |
| 52 | Home Health Care | 🏠 | 📖 | |
| 52 | Fitness Training | 🏠 | | 📖 |
| 53 | Counseling 1 | | 🏠 | 📖 |
| 54 | Accounting | 🏠 | | 🏠 |

📖 City Downtown Library     🏠 City Community Center

1. The classes meet in _____.
   - A one place
   - ● two places
   - C three places
   - D four places

2. There will be only two courses in the _____.
   - A fall
   - B winter
   - C spring
   - ● summer

3. Classes in _____ are only at the City Downtown Library.
   - ● Criminal Justice
   - B Accounting
   - C Counseling 1
   - D Home Health Care

4. Counseling 1 is on catalog page _____.
   - A 51
   - B 52
   - ● 53
   - D 54

5. Students can take _____ in the summer.
   - A Criminal Justice
   - B Fitness Training
   - C Accounting
   - ● Home Health Care

6. Which word means the same as *advising*?
   - A fitness
   - ● counseling
   - C training
   - D accounting

**2** **Complete the conversation. Write the answers.**

1. **A** What are you going to do after class?

   **B** study / at the library _I'm going to study at the library._

2. **A** What are you having for dinner tonight?

   **B** have / chicken _I'm having chicken._

3. **A** What are you going to do this evening?

   **B** watch / TV _I'm going to watch TV._

4. **A** When will you get up tomorrow?

   **B** get up / at 6:00 a.m. _I'll get up at 6:00 a.m._

5. **A** What are you doing tomorrow?

   **B** register / for a class _I'm going to register for a class._

6. **A** What classes will you take next year?

   **B** take / Criminal Justice 2 _I'll take Criminal Justice 2._

7. **A** What are you doing this weekend?

   **B** visit / friends _I'll going to visit friends._

8. **A** What will you do on your vacation?

   **B** swim / hike _I'll going to swim and hike._

9. **A** What are you going to do after graduation?

   **B** get a job _I'm going to get a job._

10. **A** What are you taking to the party?

    **B** take / flowers _I'm taking flowers._

# UNIT 3 FRIENDS AND FAMILY

## Lesson A Listening

**1** **Complete the words.**

1. s m _o_ k _e_
2. g r ___ c ___ r ___ ___ s
3. b r ___ k ___ n - d ___ w n c ___ r
4. ___ v ___ r h ___ ___ ted e ___ ___ i n ___

5. w ___ r r ___ ed m ___ n
6. t r ___ n k
7. ___ o o ___

**2** **Write the words from Exercise 1.**

5. _____

1. _____

2. _____

3. _____

4. _____

6. _____

7. _____

## 3 Listen. Complete the conversation.

**A** Hi, Miguel.

**B** Laurie? Are you OK? You sound _____*worried*_____.
   1.

**A** I'm OK, but the car ____broke down____ down.
   2.

**B** Where are you?

**A** We're near the supermarket. I bought a lot of _____. I put them in the
   3.
   _____. Then I started the car, but _____ came from
   4.   5.
   the _____.
   6.

**B** Did you open the _____?
   7.

**A** Yes. I called the mechanic, too.

**B** OK. I'll be right there.

# Lesson B  What did you do last weekend?

Study the chart on page 128.

## 1 Look at the picture and read the email. Circle the answers.

From: shin17@cup.org
To: grandma17@cup.org
Date: August 10, 2018
Subject: Picnic last week

Here's a picture from last weekend! We had a great time.

Love,
Shin

1. What did Shin do last weekend?
   a. He went to the beach.
   b. He went to the park.

2. Did he take his children?
   a. Yes, he did.
   b. No, he didn't.

3. Did he take the bus?
   a. Yes, he did.
   b. No, he didn't.

4. Did he grill hamburgers?
   a. Yes, he did.
   b. No, he didn't.

5. What did his son do?
   a. He read a book.
   b. He listened to music.

6. Did his daughter listen to music?
   a. Yes, she did.
   b. No, she didn't.

## 2 Write the simple past.

1. grill _____grilled_____
2. buy _____bought_____
3. drive _____drove_____
4. eat _____ate_____
5. fix _____fixed_____
6. go _____went_____

7. have _____had_____
8. watch _____watched_____
9. meet _____met_____
10. play _____played_____
11. read _____read_____
12. stay _____stayed_____

**3** **Complete the sentences. Use the simple past.**

1. Frankie and Claudia _____*went*_____ to the park.
   (go)
2. They ___*met*___ their friends.
   (meet)
3. They ___*played*___ soccer.
   (play)
4. They ___*had*___ a picnic dinner.
   (have)
5. They ___*ate*___ birthday cake.
   (eat)
6. They ___*drove*___ home.
   (drive)

**4** **Match the pictures with the sentences in Exercise 3.**

a. _5_

b. _4_

c. _3_

d. _2_

e. _1_

f. _6_

Study the charts on pages 126 and 128.

**1** **Complete the sentences. Use the simple present or the simple past.**

1. Anton ___went___ to English class at 7:00 last night.
   (go)

2. I usually ___watch___ movies on my computer after work.
   (watch)

3. Anita ___cleaned___ her apartment last Saturday.
   (clean)

4. Tom usually ___eats___ dinner at home.
   (eat)

5. I usually ___leave___ for work at 8:15 a.m.
   (leave)

6. Adriana ___met___ her friends after class yesterday.
   (meet)

**2** **Read Malik's datebook from last week. Match the questions with the answers.**

| Sunday | get up late! |
|---|---|
| Monday | work → 5:00<br>tennis with Geraldo 6:00 p.m. |
| Tuesday | 8:00 ESL class before work<br>work → 5:00 |
| Wednesday | work → 5:00<br>Reza's soccer game 5:30 |
| Thursday | 8:00 ESL class<br>work → 5:00<br>birthday dinner at Mom and Dad's at 7:00 |
| Friday | leave work early<br>citizenship class at 4:00 |
| Saturday | tennis with Geraldo 9:00 a.m. |

1. When does Malik usually finish work? __d__
2. What day did Malik finish work early last week? __g__
3. What did Malik have at 4:00 on Friday? __e__
4. When did Malik sleep late? __b__
5. Did Malik play tennis with Geraldo on Monday? __f__
6. Where did Malik eat dinner last Thursday? __c__
7. What days does Malik have ESL class? __a__
8. What day did Malik watch Reza's soccer game? __h__

√a. Tuesday and Thursday.
√b. On Sunday.
√c. At his parents' house.
√d. At 5:00.
√e. A citizenship class.
√f. No, he didn't.
√g. On Friday.
√h. On Wednesday.

**3** **Complete the sentences. Use the simple present or the simple past.**

1. Malik ___*has*___ an ESL class on Tuesday and Thursday.
   (have)

2. Malik usually ___*plays*___ tennis with Geraldo on Monday and Saturday.
   (play)

3. Malik ___*worked*___ until 7:00 last Tuesday.
   (work)

4. Malik ___*has*___ a citizenship class every Friday at 4:00.
   (have)

5. Malik and Geraldo ___*met*___ for tennis at 9:00 last Saturday morning.
   (meet)

6. Malik usually ___*gets*___ up late on Sunday.
   (get)

7. Malik and his wife and children usually ___*eat*___ dinner at home.
   (eat)

8. They ___*ate*___ dinner at his parents' house last Thursday.
   (eat)

**4** **Read the Lopez family's calendar. Answer the questions.**

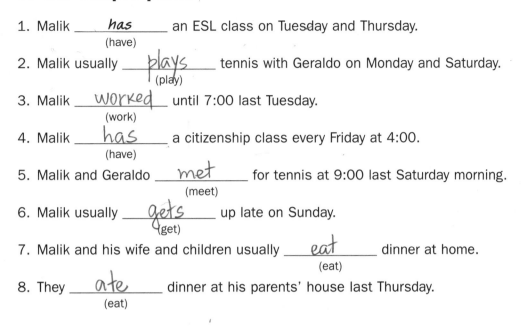

| Monday | Tuesday | Wednesday | Thursday | Friday |
|---|---|---|---|---|
| Melissa – movie with Uncle Jaime | Tony – meet friends after work 6:00 | Victor – study for English test | Mom and Dad – buy groceries | Mom – take English exam<br>Tony – meet friends after work 5:30 |

1. When do Mom and Dad usually buy groceries?
   *They usually buy groceries on Thursday.*

2. When did Mom take her English exam?
   *She took her English exam on friday.*

3. What does Tony usually do after work on Tuesday and Friday?
   *He usually meets friends.*

4. When did Melissa go to a movie with her uncle?
   *She goes to a movie with her uncle on Monday.*

5. What time did Tony meet his friends last Friday?
   *He met his friends last friday at 5:30.*

6. What did Victor do last Wednesday?
   *He studied for English class.*

# Lesson D  Reading

**1**  **Read and circle the correct answers. Then listen.**

August 10

   Today was a great day. This morning, the children helped
me. Ron did the dishes, Lisa made the beds, and Sonia did
the laundry. The children are usually busy on the weekend,
and Ed usually works. They don't have time to help me. But
not today!
   At noon, Ed made lunch for us. Lunch was delicious.
After lunch, I had a great afternoon. First, I took a long
bath. Then, I took a long nap. I usually go shopping in the
afternoon, but not today. After my nap, I got up and got
dressed. Then, I made dinner. After dinner, we all watched
a movie on TV. Now it's time for bed. What a great day!

1. Who helped Ana today?
   a. Ron
   b. Lisa
   c. Sonia
   d. all of the above

2. Who did the dishes?
   a. Ed
   b. Lisa
   c. Ron
   d. Sonia

3. Who made the beds?
   a. Ed
   b. Lisa
   c. Ron
   d. Sonia

4. Who did the laundry?
   a. Ed
   b. Lisa
   c. Ron
   d. Sonia

5. Who made lunch?
   a. Ed
   b. Lisa
   c. Ron
   d. Sonia

6. Who usually helps Ana?
   a. Ana's friends
   b. the children
   c. Ed
   d. none of the above

7. Who took a long bath and a long nap?
   a. Ana
   b. the children
   c. Ed
   d. all of the above

8. Why was today a great day?
   a. Ana's family helped her.
   b. Ana went shopping.
   c. Lisa did the laundry.
   d. Sonia made the beds.

**2** **Complete the chart.**

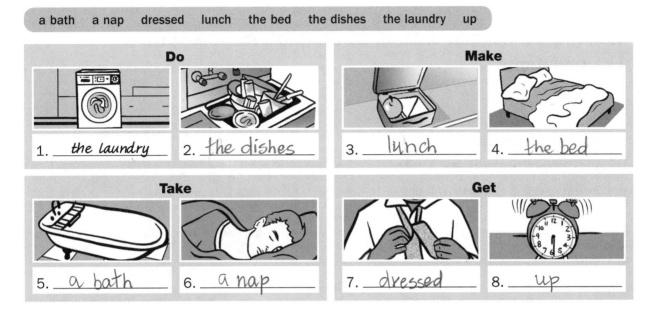

a bath    a nap    dressed    lunch    the bed    the dishes    the laundry    up

**Do**

1. _the laundry_    2. _the dishes_

**Make**

3. _lunch_    4. _the bed_

**Take**

5. _a bath_    6. _a nap_

**Get**

7. _dressed_    8. _up_

**3** **Read the conversation. Write *do*, *get*, *make*, or *take* in the simple present or simple past. Then listen.**

**Mom**   Sonia, did you ____make____ the beds this morning?
                         1.

**Sonia**  No, I didn't, Mom. I ____got____ up late today. But I always make the beds.
                         2.
           It's Ron's turn.

**Ron**    Mom, I can't make the beds. I don't have time. And I always ____do____ the
                         3.
           dishes. It's Lisa's turn.

**Lisa**   OK, Mom. In a minute.

**Mom**   Ron, did you ____do____ the dishes this morning?
                         4.

**Ron**    Yes, I ____did____.
                         5.

**Mom**   And what about your homework?

**Ron**    I ____did____ my homework yesterday. Today is Saturday.
                         6.

**Mom**   OK. Did Dad ____do____ the laundry this morning?
                         7.

**Sonia**  No, Mom. He always ____takes____ a nap on Saturday.
                         8.

**Mom**   A nap! It's 9:00 a.m.!

# Lesson E Writing

**1** **Read Ana's schedule. Look at the picture. Answer the questions.**

*Usually*

### My Morning Schedule

6:00:  Get up and take a bath.

6:15:  Get Ed up and get dressed.

6:30:  Get Sonia up and then make the children's lunches for school.

6:45:  Get Ron up and then make my lunch.

7:10:  Get Lisa up and then eat my breakfast.

7:15:  Make the children's beds.

7:20:  Ed leaves for work.

7:30:  Children leave for school.

7:45:  Do the dishes.

7:55:  Leave for work.

*This morning*

1. Who usually gets up first?

   Ana usually gets up first.

2. Who got up first this morning?

   Ed got up first this morning.

3. Who usually takes a bath every morning?

   Ana usually takes a bath every morning.

4. Who didn't take a bath this morning?

   Ana didn't take a bath this morning.

5. Who usually leaves for work at 7:20?

   Ed usually leaves for work at 7:20.

6. Who usually leaves for school at 7:30?

   Children usually leave for school at 7:30.

**2** Answer the questions. Use Ana's schedule in Exercise 1.

1. When does Ana get up? _She gets up at 6:00._
2. When does Ana get dressed? _She gets dressed at 6:15._
3. When does Ana eat her breakfast? _She eats her breakfast at 7:10._
4. When does Ana do the dishes? _She does the dishes at 7:45._
5. When does Ana make the children's beds? _She makes the children's beds at 7:15._
6. When does Ana leave the house? _____

**3** Read the sentences. Write *First*, *Next*, or *Finally* on the correct line.

1. Last Monday, I had a very bad morning.
   _Next_ , I didn't have time for breakfast.
   _First_ , I woke up late.
   _Finally_ , I was late for work.

2. Last Sunday, my family went to the beach.
   _Finally_ , we drove home for dinner.
   _First_ , we had a picnic lunch.
   _Next_ , we relaxed all afternoon.

**4** Write the sentences from Exercise 3 in the correct order.

1. _Last Monday, I had a very bad morning. First, I woke up late. Next, I didn't have time for breakfast. Finally, I was late for work._

2. _Last Sunday, my family went to the beach. First, we had a picnic lunch. Next, we relaxed all afternoon. Finally, we drove home for dinner._

**1** **Read the questions. Look at the ad. Fill in the correct answers.**

**JACKSON REPAIR**

Next to the supermarket on Washington Street  (973) 555-1850

- We fix car problems from hood to trunk!
- SUMMER REPAIR SPECIAL: 20% off!
- ENGINE SPECIAL: $150
- BROKEN-DOWN CAR?
  We'll bring you home! $50

OPEN MONDAY-SATURDAY 8:00 a.m.–6:00 p.m.

1. How much is the Engine Special?
   - (A) $50
   - (B) $100
   - (●) $150
   - (D) $200

2. What is the Jackson Repair phone number?
   - (A) 20%
   - (B) $50
   - (C) $150
   - (D) (973) 555-1850

3. What is the Summer Repair Special?
   - (A) 20% off
   - (B) $50 off
   - (C) 50% off
   - (D) $150 off

4. When is Jackson Repair open?
   - (A) 6:00 a.m.–8:00 p.m.
   - (B) 6:00 p.m.–8:00 p.m.
   - (C) 8:00 a.m.–6:00 p.m.
   - (D) 8:00 p.m.–6:00 a.m.

5. Where is Jackson Repair?
   - (A) at home
   - (B) on Jackson Street
   - (C) in the supermarket
   - (D) on Washington Street

6. What word or phrase means *stopped working*?
   - (A) fixed
   - (B) broken down
   - (C) repaired
   - (D) problems

**2** **Complete the story about the Ramirez family's weekend schedule. Use *do, make, play,* or *go.***

| The Ramirez Family's Weekend Schedule | | | |
|---|---|---|---|
| **Grandma Rosa** | **Jorge & Sara** | **Lorena** | **Daniel** |
| • Cookies for the family on Saturday morning<br>• Cards with the Lings on Saturday night<br>• Dinner for the family on Sunday | • Housework on Saturday morning<br>• Dancing at the club on Saturday night<br>• Breakfast for the family on Sunday morning | • Soccer on Saturday morning<br>• Shopping on Saturday afternoon<br>• Homework on Sunday afternoon | • Basketball on Friday night<br>• Chores on Saturday morning<br>• Computer games on Saturday night |

The Ramirez family is very busy on the weekend. On Saturday morning, Grandma

Rosa _____*makes cookies*_____ for the family. On Saturday night, she usually
　　　　　　　1.

_____ with the Lings. She _____ for the family on
　　　　　2.　　　　　　　　　　　　　　　　　　　　3.

Sunday. Jorge and Sara _____ on Saturday morning. They usually
　　　　　　　　　　　　　　　4.

_____ on Saturday night, and they _____ for the
　　　　　5.　　　　　　　　　　　　　　　　　　　　　　6.

family on Sunday morning. On Saturday morning, Lorena _____.
　　　　　　　　　　　　　　　　　　　　　　　　　　　　　7.

On Saturday afternoon, she usually _____ for groceries. She
　　　　　　　　　　　　　　　　　8.

_____ on Sunday afternoon. Daniel _____ on Friday
　　　　　9.　　　　　　　　　　　　　　　　　　　　　10.

night. He _____ on Saturday morning, and he _____
　　　　　　　　11.　　　　　　　　　　　　　　　　　　　　　　　　　12.

on Saturday night.

# UNIT 4 HEALTH

## Lesson A Listening

**1** **Complete the words.**

1. i n j u r __e__ d  h ____ n d
2. c r ____ t c h ____ s
3. s p r a ____ n ____ d  ____ n k l ____
4. b r ____ k ____ n  b ____ n ____
5. ____ n h ____ l ____ r
6. X - r ____ ____
7. p ____ i n f ____ l  k n ____ ____

**2** **Look at the picture. Write the words from Exercise 1.**

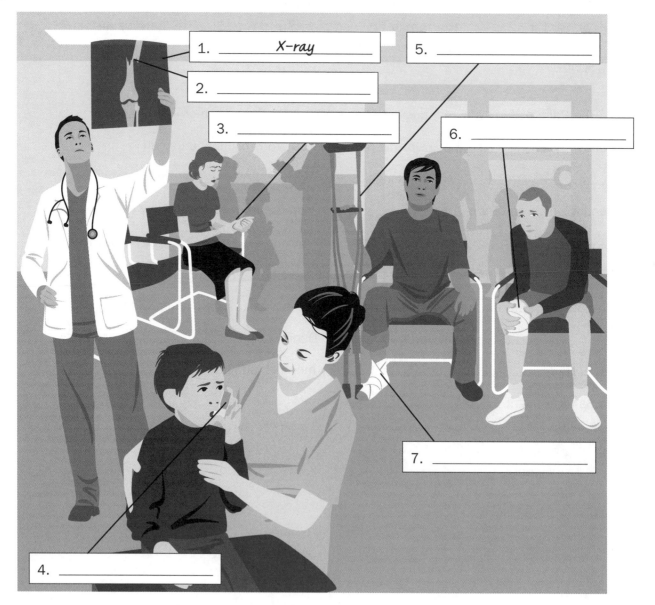

1. _____X-ray_____
2. _____
3. _____
4. _____
5. _____
6. _____
7. _____

**3** **Complete the story. Use the words from Exercise 1.**

It's a busy day at the hospital. A man had an accident at work. He has a ___*sprained*___

ankle. He can't walk. He needs _____ . A woman had an accident, too. Now she
                                        2.

has an _____ hand. The doctor is looking at an _____ . It's a picture of a
                3.                                                    4.

_____ bone. The nurse is helping a little boy. She gives him an _____ .
        5.                                                                            6.

**4** **Listen. Circle the correct answers.**

**Conversation A**

1. Who had an accident?
   a. Ricardo
   b. Susanna
   c. the children

2. Where did the accident happen?
   a. at work
   b. at home
   c. at school

3. Where will Susanna go after the
   phone call?
   a. to the hospital
   b. to work
   c. to school

**Conversation B**

4. Where is Susanna right now?
   a. at home
   b. at work
   c. at the hospital

5. What happened to Susanna?
   a. She sprained her ankle.
   b. She broke her arm.
   c. She broke her leg.

6. Where is the hospital?
   a. on Pine Street
   b. on 15th Street
   c. on 50th Street

# Lesson B You should go to the hospital.

Study the chart on page 129.

## 1 Circle *should* or *shouldn't*.

1. Karl's tooth hurts. He (should) / shouldn't go to the dentist.

2. The children are all sick. They **should** / **shouldn't** go to school today.

3. My eyes hurt. I **should** / **shouldn't** watch TV right now.

4. Your leg is very sore. You **should** / **shouldn't** get an X-ray.

5. Mario hurt his back. He **should** / **shouldn't** see a doctor.

6. We ate a big lunch. We **should** / **shouldn't** eat a big dinner.

## 2 Complete the sentences. Use *should* or *shouldn't*.

1. **A** Uncle Pete has a bottle of medicine.

   **B** He ___*shouldn't*___ keep it in a hot place.

   He ___*should*___ keep it away from children.

2. **A** Sue has a headache.

   **B** She _____ listen to loud music.

   She _____ take some aspirin.

3. **A** Abel has a stomachache.

   **B** He _____ take some medicine.

   He _____ eat his lunch.

4. **A** Francine has a sprained ankle.

   **B** She _____ play soccer.

   She _____ get a pair of crutches.

5. **A** I'm very hot. I don't feel well.

   **B** You _____ drink a lot of water.

   You _____ stay in the sun.

6. **A** Mrs. Lam hurt her leg.

   **B** She _____ see a doctor.

   She _____ walk.

**3** **Complete the sentences.**

break   clothes   shade   sun   towel   water

You're working outside. It's very hot. What should you do? What shouldn't you do?

✓ You shouldn't wear heavy ____clothes____ .
   1.

✓ You should take a _____ and drink a lot of _____ .
   2.                                          3.

✓ You should use a wet _____ .
   4.

✓ You shouldn't stay in the _____ . You should stay in the _____ .
   5.                                                              6.

**4** **Complete the sentences. Use *should* or *shouldn't*.**

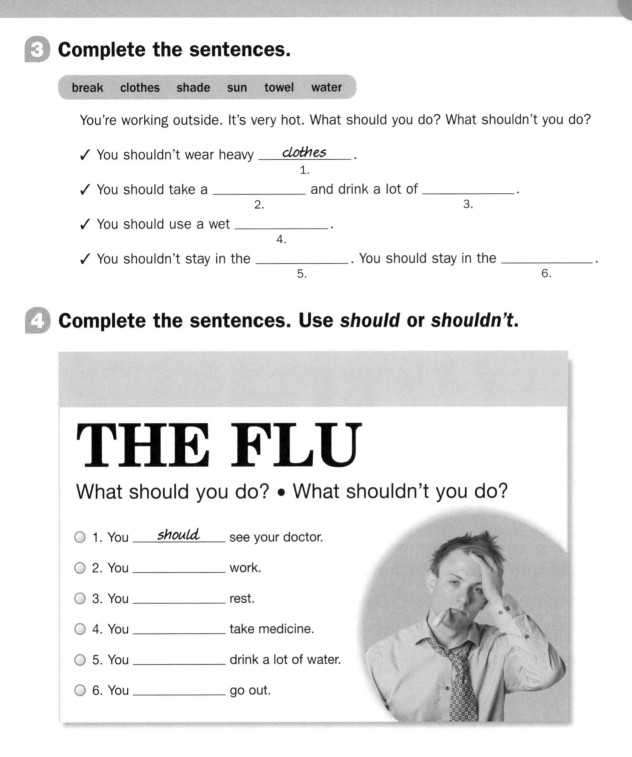

# THE FLU

## What should you do? • What shouldn't you do?

◯ 1. You ____should____ see your doctor.

◯ 2. You _____ work.

◯ 3. You _____ rest.

◯ 4. You _____ take medicine.

◯ 5. You _____ drink a lot of water.

◯ 6. You _____ go out.

Study the chart on page 127.

**1** **Complete the conversations. Use *have to* or *has to*. Then listen.**

1. **A** Linda hurt her hand. What does she have to do?

   **B** She ____*has to*____ see a doctor.

2. **A** Rod hurt his back. What does he have to do?

   **B** He _____ stay home today.

3. **A** Jimmy broke his arm. What do we have to do?

   **B** We _____ take Jimmy to the hospital.

4. **A** I have a headache. What do I have to do?

   **B** You _____ go home early.

5. **A** Tim broke his leg. What does he have to do?

   **B** He _____ use these crutches.

6. **A** Jerry and Charlie have asthma. What do they have to do?

   **B** They _____ take their medicine.

**2** **Answer the questions. Use *have to* or *has to*.**

1. Jesse sprained his ankle. What does he have to do?

   (use crutches) ____*He has to use crutches.*____

2. Mari burned her hand. What does she have to do?

   (see the doctor) _____

3. Irvin broke his arm. What does he have to do?

   (get an X-ray) _____

4. Elian hurt his hand at work. What does he have to do?

   (fill out an accident report) _____

5. Rosa has a headache. What does she have to do?

   (take medicine) _____

**3** **Match the sentences with the labels.**

1. You have to take this in the morning.  ___c___

2. You have to keep this in the refrigerator.  _____

3. You have to eat when you take this.  _____

4. You have to use this at night.  _____

5. You have to keep this out of the refrigerator.  _____

6. You have to use this in your eye.  _____

a  ◎ FOR THE eye

b  DO NOT Refrigerate

c  TAKE IN THE MORNING

d  TAKE WITH FOOD OR MILK

e  BEDTIME

f  Refrigerate

**4** **Complete the conversation.**

| do | food | have | medicine | morning | prescription | refrigerator | to |
|----|------|------|----------|---------|--------------|--------------|-----|

**A** Here's your ___prescription___, Mrs. Lopez.
               1.

**B** Thanks. What _____ I have to do?
                    2.

**A** You _____ keep this _____ in the _____ .
         3.                      4.                  5.

**B** OK. Can I take it in the _____ ?
                              6.

**A** Yes, and you have to take it with _____ .
                                        7.

**B** I see. I'll take it with my breakfast. Thank you, Dr. Simmons.

# Lesson D Reading

**1** **Read and circle the correct answers. Then listen.**

## KNOW YOUR BLOOD PRESSURE

Are you over 21? Yes? Your doctor should check your blood pressure every year. High blood pressure can be dangerous. Here are some ways to lower your blood pressure. First, try to change your lifestyle:

- Stop smoking
- Lose weight.
- Exercise every day.
- Eat lots of fruits and vegetables. Don't eat a lot of fat.
- Don't use a lot of salt. Don't drink a lot of coffee.
- Reduce your stress.

Second, talk to your doctor about your blood pressure. Maybe you need to take medicine. Talk to your doctor! Start today!

1. What should you do to lower your blood pressure?
   a. change your lifestyle
   b. drink coffee
   c. eat fat
   d. use salt

2. You have high blood pressure. What should you eat?
   a. fat
   b. fruits
   c. salt
   d. none of the above

3. You need to lower your blood pressure. What should you do?
   a. drink coffee
   b. start smoking
   c. eat healthy foods
   d. use salt

4. You need to change your diet. What should you do?
   a. drink coffee
   b. eat vegetables
   c. exercise
   d. take medicine

5. Why should a doctor check your blood pressure every year?
   a. to make sure you are healthy
   b. to reduce your stress
   c. to make you exercise more
   d. none of the above

6. What is the purpose of the warning?
   a. to make people exercise
   b. to tell people to stop drinking coffee
   c. to make doctors happy
   d. to help people be more healthy

## 2 Match the words.

1. a swollen  _d_          a. neck
2. high blood ____         b. wrist
3. a sprained ____         c. pains
4. a stiff ____            d. knee
5. chest ____              e. pressure

## 3 Look at the pictures. Write sentences. Use *has* or *have*.

1. ___She has a rash.___
   _____

2. _____
   _____

3. _____
   _____

4. _____
   _____

5. _____
   _____

6. _____
   _____

## 4 Complete the sentences.

> accident   chest   cut   hurt   medicine

- Did someone get ___hurt___?
  1.
- Was there a bad _____?
  2.
- Does someone have _____ pains?
  3.
- Does someone have a bad _____?
  4.
- Did a child take your _____?
  5.

## EMERGENCY? CALL 911

# Lesson E Writing

**1** **Read the questions. Look at the form. Answer the questions.**

### Sleepy Burgers: Accident Log                                   August 2018

| Employee | Job | Date | Where | Injury |
|----------|-----|------|-------|--------|
| J. Haddan | Server | 8-3-13 | Dining Room | Sprained ankle |
| M. Almaleh | Cook | 8-10-13 | Kitchen | Burned hand |
| F. Engels | Cook | 8-12-13 | Kitchen | Cut hand |
| E. Perry | Hostess | 8-20-13 | Dining Room | Sprained wrist |

**Problems? Call the U.S. Department of Labor at (800) 555-0810.**

1. How many accidents were there at the restaurant in August?

   *There were four accidents in August.*

2. Who had a sprained ankle?

   _____

3. When did the cook burn his hand?

   _____

4. What did Mr. Engels cut?

   _____

5. What was Ms. Perry's injury?

   _____

6. What is the name of the restaurant?

   _____

**2** **Number the sentences in the correct order.**

1. Yesterday, I cut my hand.

   _____ The knife slipped.

   _1_ I was cooking dinner.

   _____ My hands were wet.

2. Yesterday, I burned my leg.

   _____ My son ran into the table.

   _____ I was eating hot soup.

   _____ The table fell over.

## 3 Complete the sentences.

accident    days      injuries    shouldn't
burned      has to    medicine    work

**Cottage Hospital**

**Report**

I treated Carlos Garcia today, 5/09/2018, for ___burned___ hands.
1.

He got these _____ at work at Fast Frank's Restaurant this
2.

afternoon. He says it was an _____.
3.

**Recommendations**

1. Carlos _____ take one ounce of this _____
4.                                              5.

every four hours for ten _____.
6.

2. Carlos _____ work for one week. He can return
7.

to _____ on May 16, 2018.
8.

**Signature** _William Crawford M.D._

**Date** _May 9, 2018_

## 4 Answer the questions. Use the report in Exercise 3.

1. Who was hurt?

_Carlos Garcia was hurt._

2. What was his injury?

3. When was he hurt?

4. Was it an accident?

5. When can he return to work?

6. What is the name of the restaurant?

# Lesson F Another view

**1 Read the questions. Look at the bar graph. Fill in the correct answers.**

## WORKPLACE INJURIES FOR EVERY 100 WORKERS IN 2015

construction
farming
computer factories
nursing
clothing stores

0  1  2  3  4  5  6  7  8  9  10  11  12

Source: U.S. Bureau of Labor Statistics, 2015

1. What year is this bar graph for?
   - A  2017
   - B  2005
   - ● 2015
   - D  2013

2. For every 100 workers, which workplace had 12 injuries?
   - A  construction
   - B  farming
   - C  nursing
   - D  clothing stores

3. For every 100 workers, which workplace had three and a half injuries?
   - A  farming
   - B  nursing
   - C  clothing stores
   - D  construction

4. For every 100 workers, how many injuries happened on farms?
   - A  5
   - B  almost 4
   - C  almost 6
   - D  9

5. For every 100 workers, how many injuries happened in clothing stores?
   - A  about 2
   - B  3
   - C  over 6
   - D  9

6. Which workplace had the most injuries?
   - A  nursing
   - B  clothing stores
   - C  construction
   - D  farming

**2 Complete the sentences.**

doctor   drowsiness   product   tablets

1. Do not take more than 8 _____*tablets*_____ in 24 hours.

2. Ask a _____ before use if you have liver or kidney disease.

3. When using this _____ , do not take more than directed.

4. This medicine can cause _____ .

**52** UNIT 4

**3** **Read the label. Match the words in Column 1 with the words in Column 2. Then complete the sentences with** *have to / must*, *must not*, **or** *don't have to*.

Directions :
Take two pills three times a day.
Take with or without water.
Do NOT take with food.
Do not lie down after taking medication.
Do NOT give medication to children under 12 years old.
Refrigerate medication.

**Column 1**

1. have to / must

2. must not

3. don't have to

**Column 2**

a. take the pills three times a day

b. refrigerate this medication

c. give this medication to an eight-year-old

d. take six pills a day

e. lie down after you take this medication

f. take this medication with water

1. You _____*have to / must*_____ take the pills three times a day.

2. You _____ refrigerate this medication.

3. You _____ give this medication to an eight-year-old.

4. You _____ take six pills a day.

5. You _____ lie down after you take this medication.

6. You _____ take this medication with water.

# UNIT 5 AROUND TOWN

## Lesson A Listening

**1** **Complete the words.**

1. a s _u_ _i_ t c _a_ s _e_
2. an ___ n f ___ r m ___ t ___ ___ n d ___ s k
3. a w ___ ___ t ___ n g ___ r ___ ___
4. a t r ___ c k
5. a t ___ c k ___ t b ___ ___ t h
6. d ___ p ___ r t ___ r ___ s
7. a r r ___ v ___ l s

**2** **Look at the picture. Write the words from Exercise 1.**

1. _____a ticket booth_____

4. _____

2. _____

5. _____

6. _____

3. _____

7. _____

## 3 Match the actions with the pictures.

a.

b.

c.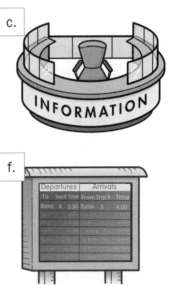

d.

e.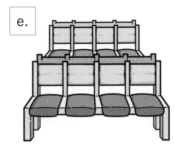

f.

_b_ 1. You put your clothes in this.

_____ 2. Your train leaves from here.

_____ 3. You look for train times here.

_____ 4. You ask questions here.

_____ 5. You buy your ticket here.

_____ 6. You can sit here to wait for your train.

## 4 Listen. Circle T (True) or F (False).

**Conversation A**

1. The next train for Philadelphia will leave at 5:20.  T  (F)

2. Oscar and Lily need to get train information.  T  F

3. The information booth is next to Track 1.  T  F

**Conversation B**

4. Trains leave for Philadelphia every half hour.  T  F

5. Oscar and Lily will take the 10:20 train.  T  F

6. The 10:20 train leaves from Track 5.  T  F

**Conversation C**

7. Two tickets to Philadelphia cost $100.  T  F

8. It takes an hour and 30 minutes to get to Philadelphia on the 10:20 train.  T  F

9. Oscar usually goes to Philadelphia by train.  T  F

# Lesson B How often? How long?

**1** **Read the questions. Look at the train schedule. Circle the correct answers.**

| Los Angeles Unity Station<br>Pacific Express – San Diego to Los Angeles | | |
|---|---|---|
| **MONDAY THROUGH FRIDAY** | | |
| Departs San Diego | Arrives Los Angeles | Duration |
| 12:10 p.m. | 2:55 p.m. | 2 H 45 M |
| 3:10 p.m. | 5:55 p.m. | 2 H 45 M |
| 6:10 p.m. | 9:10 p.m. | 3 H |
| 9:10 p.m. | 1:25 a.m. | 4 H 15 M |
| **SATURDAY AND SUNDAY** | | |
| 6:45 a.m. | 9:45 a.m. | 3 H |
| 2:26 p.m. | 4:26 p.m. | 2 H |
| 6:10 p.m. | 9:35 p.m. | 3 H 25 M |

1. How often does the train go from San Diego to Los Angeles on the weekend?
   a. three times a day
   b. four times a day
   c. ten times a day

2. How long does it take to go from San Diego to Los Angeles on the 3:10 p.m. train?
   a. two hours and 45 minutes
   b. three hours
   c. four hours and 10 minutes

3. How often does the train go from San Diego to Los Angeles on weekdays?
   a. three times a day
   b. four times a day
   c. seven times a day

4. How long does it take to go from San Diego to Los Angeles on the 6:45 a.m. train on the weekend?
   a. two hours
   b. two hours and 25 minutes
   c. three hours

## 2 Match the questions with the answers. Use the schedule in Exercise 1.

1. How often do trains go from San Diego to Los Angeles on weekdays? __f__

2. How long does it take to go to Los Angeles on the 9:10 p.m. train? _____

3. How often do you take the train to Los Angeles? _____

4. How long does it take to drive from San Diego to Los Angeles? _____

5. How often do the trains go to Los Angeles on the weekend? _____

6. How long does it take to go to Los Angeles on the Saturday afternoon train? _____

a. It takes four hours and 15 minutes.

b. I take the train there once or twice a month.

c. It takes two hours.

d. They go to Los Angeles three times a day.

e. It takes a long time to drive there.

f. They go every three hours.

## 3 Read the chart and write the questions. Then listen.

|  | How often? | How long? |
| --- | --- | --- |
| drive to the beach | twice a month | one hour |
| walk to the park | three or four times a week | half an hour |
| go downtown by bus | every day | 45 minutes |

1. **A** _How often do you drive to the beach?_ _____

   **B** Twice a month.

   **A** _How long does it take?_ _____

   **B** About one hour.

2. **A** _____

   **B** About three or four times a week.

   **A** _____

   **B** About half an hour.

3. **A** _____

   **B** Every day.

   **A** _____

   **B** About 45 minutes.

# Lesson C She often walks to school.

**1** **Put the words in order by frequency.**

always   never   often   rarely   sometimes

0% ◄─────────────────────────────────────────► 100%

1. ____*never*____ 2. _____ 3. _____ 4. _____ 5. _____

**2** **Read the chart. Complete the sentences. Use the words from Exercise 1.**

| **English 201** September–October | **Number of classes:** 45 |
| --- | --- |
| **Name** | **Number of times late** |
| Wang-jie | 40 |
| Ayuko | 37 |
| Diana | 0 |
| Arturo | 3 |
| Marisol | 45 |
| Pedro | 20 |

1. Ayuko is ____*often*____ late for class.

2. Ayuko _____ arrives on time.

3. Marisol is _____ late for class.

4. Marisol _____ arrives on time.

5. Diana is _____ on time for class.

6. Diana _____ arrives late.

7. Pedro is _____ late for class.

8. Pedro _____ arrives on time.

9. Arturo _____ arrives late.

10. Arturo is _____ on time.

11. Wang-jie is _____ late.

12. Wang-jie _____ arrives on time.

**Read the chart. Answer the questions.**

| Edwin | Never | Rarely | Usually | Always |
|---|---|---|---|---|
| walks to school | | | | ✓ |
| drives to school | ✓ | | | |
| eats lunch at 1:00 p.m. | | ✓ | | |
| eats dinner at home | | | ✓ | |
| goes to sleep at 10:00 p.m. | | | ✓ | |

1. **A** How often does Edwin walk to school?

   **B** *He always walks to school.*

2. **A** How often does Edwin drive to school?

   **B** _____

3. **A** How often does Edwin eat lunch at 1:00 p.m.?

   **B** _____

4. **A** How often does Edwin eat dinner at home?

   **B** _____

5. **A** How often does Edwin go to sleep at 10:00 p.m.?

   **B** _____

## 4 Read the sentences. Circle *Yes* or *No*.

1. Linda goes out to a restaurant about twice a year.

   a. Linda rarely goes out to a restaurant.   (Yes)   No

   b. Linda always eats at home.   Yes   No

2. Fred's car is very old. It often breaks down. Fred takes the bus to work when his car is broken down. He drives his car to work when it is fixed.

   a. Fred never drives to work.   Yes   No

   b. Fred often takes the bus.   Yes   No

3. Our favorite lunch place is Sam's Sandwich Shop. We go there about three times a week. On the other days, we bring our lunch from home.

   a. We always eat lunch out.   Yes   No

   b. We sometimes bring our lunch.   Yes   No

# Lesson D  Reading

**1** **Read and circle the correct answers. Then listen.**

Dear Nina,

    We're having a wonderful time in Miami. We always have a lot of fun here. We usually stay with Mariam's relatives, but they're not here right now. This time we're staying at a hotel. We usually come to Miami two or three times a year. Layla always wants to go shopping at Miami International Mall. She likes to buy souvenirs there. Ali never wants to go shopping. He wants to go swimming. Mariam and I like to go sightseeing, but the children rarely go with us. I always take a lot of pictures. We'll show you our pictures next week!

Love from us,

Khalid

1. Khalid and his family ____ go to Miami.
   a. never
   b. rarely
   c. often
   d. always

2. ____ always wants to go shopping.
   a. Ali
   b. Khalid
   c. Layla
   d. Mariam

3. Khalid always ____.
   a. goes shopping
   b. goes sightseeing
   c. goes swimming
   d. takes a lot of pictures

4. Khalid and Mariam rarely ____.
   a. go sightseeing together
   b. go sightseeing with the children
   c. stay with Mariam's relatives
   d. take pictures

**2** **Circle the answers. Use the information in Exercise 1.**

1. The name of Khalid's wife is **Mariam** / **Layla**.

2. Khalid and his family are staying **with relatives** / **at a hotel**.

3. Khalid and his family **know** / **don't know** Miami very well.

4. Khalid and **Layla** / **Mariam** go sightseeing together.

**3** **Complete the sentences. Use the correct form of the verbs in the box.**

buy   go   stay   take   write

1. Lee usually _____*goes*_____ swimming on Saturday afternoon.
2. Ralph sometimes _____ with relatives in San Francisco.
3. Jon always _____ pictures when he's on vacation.
4. Do you like to _____ sightseeing in a new place?
5. My son rarely wants to _____ shopping with me.
6. I often _____ souvenirs when I'm on vacation.
7. How many suitcases do you usually _____ with you?
8. Don't forget to _____ postcards to me from New York City.
9. Marco sometimes _____ at a hotel when he travels.

**4** **Number the sentences in the correct order. Then write the conversation below.**

_____ It usually takes about three hours by plane.

_____ Where do you usually go?

_____ I go on vacation once a year.

_____ Oh, yes! It takes two days by car.

_____ How long does it take to get there?

__1__ How often do you go on vacation?

_____ Do you always go by plane?

_____ I usually go to Denver to see my parents.

A _How often do you go on vacation?_ _____

B _____

A _____

B _____

A _____

B _____

A _____

B _____

# Lesson E Writing

## 1 Write the questions.

1. go to / Miami / How often / trains / do / ?
   _How often do trains go to Miami?_

2. does / it / San Francisco / How long / take / to get to / ?
   _____

3. to drive to / take / does / it / Detroit / How long / ?
   _____

4. go to / does / the bus / How often / Boston / ?
   _____

5. do / you / your relatives / visit / How often / in Houston / ?
   _____

6. do / stay / you / Where / usually / ?
   _____

## 2 Write the number of the question from Exercise 1 next to the correct answer.

a. Once or twice a year. _5_

b. They go every hour. _____

c. It goes three times a day. _____

d. We always stay with my relatives. _____

e. It takes about seven hours. _____

f. It takes about two hours by car. _____

## 3 Write the durations.

| Start | Stop | |
|-------|------|---|
| 12:00 | 1:05 | 1. _one hour and five minutes_ |
| 8:00 | 9:45 | 2. |
| 9:00 | 9:09 | 3. |
| 4:00 | 5:07 | 4. |
| 4:30 | 5:00 | 5. |
| 6:00 | 7:12 | 6. |

**4** **Read and answer the questions. Then listen.**

### Liz's Life

Liz lives in San Antonio, Texas. Every year, Liz goes to Denver to see her mother and father. She usually stays in Denver for about a week. Liz misses her parents. She rarely has time off from work to visit them. But Liz has a very good job in San Antonio. She works as a receptionist in a printing company. She is very happy there.

1. How often does Liz visit her parents? _____

2. How long does she usually stay in Denver? _____

3. How often does Liz have time off from work? _____

4. How does Liz feel about her job in San Antonio? _____

**5** **Complete the story.**

Martin usually ____*goes*____ to work by
          1. go
train. It _____ about 30 minutes to
          2. take
get to work by train. Martin _____ his
                              3. leave
house at 7:15 a.m. He usually _____ to
                              4. get
work at 8:00. He _____ to be late for
                  5. not like
work. Sometimes the trains _____ late.
                            6. be
Martin _____ his laptop computer on
       7. use
the train. He rarely _____ on the train
                     8. sleep
in the morning. Sometimes he _____ a
                              9. take
nap on the trip home. He never _____
                               10. talk
to people on the train. Martin _____
                               11. like
the train. He _____ to drive to work.
              12. not like

## Lesson F  Another view

**1** **Write the question. Find the answer in the chart. Then write the answer.**

### How Students Get to School Each Morning

| Name | Transportation | Why | Duration | Arrival at school |
|---|---|---|---|---|
| Mai | | ■ Goes every half hour<br>■ Cheap | ■ 10 minutes to bus stop<br>■ 10 minutes on bus | ■ Usually 10 minutes early<br>■ Sometimes late |
| Shen-hui | | ■ No waiting<br>■ Good exercise | ■ 20 minutes | ■ Always on time |
| Phillipe | | ■ No waiting<br>■ Good exercise | ■ 35 minutes | ■ Always on time |
| Sara | | ■ Goes every 5 minutes<br>■ Usually on time | ■ 15 minutes to subway<br>■ 7 minutes on subway | ■ Rarely late |
| Zoe | | ■ No waiting | ■ 7 minutes in car<br>■ 2–15 minutes to park car | ■ Often 5 minutes late |

1. How often / bus / go  _How often does the bus go?_
   _It goes every half hour._

2. How / Shen-hui / get to school _____

   _____

3. How long / to get / from Shen-hui's house / to school / by bicycle _____

   _____

4. How often / Phillipe / arrive on time _____

   _____

5. How long / to get / from Sara's house / to school / by subway _____

   _____

6. How / Zoe / get to school _____

   _____

**2** **Complete the sentences. Use *to* or *to the*. If neither is correct, write *X*.**

1. What time do you go __*to*__ to school, Bao?

2. The crosstown bus goes _____ shopping mall.

3. We're going _____ home after the movie.

4. Jane likes her new job at the pizza restaurant. She goes _____ work right after school.

5. What is the easiest way to get _____ airport from here?

**3** **Look at the pictures. Complete the sentences. Answer the question with a place. Use *to*, *to the*, or place without *to* or *to the*.**

> bank   library   mall   outside   upstairs   work

1.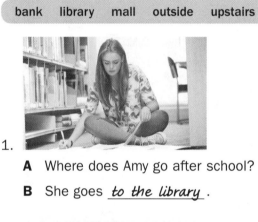
   **A** Where does Amy go after school?
   **B** She goes *to the library* .

2.
   **A** Where is Devi going?
   **B** He's going _____ .

3.
   **A** I need to get money for my bills.
   **B** You should go _____ .

4.
   **A** Where is Tina going in such a hurry?
   **B** She's going _____ . She's late!

5.
   **A** I like to stay home most of the time.
   **B** Not me! I go _____ on nice days like today.

6.
   **A** Where are your friends going on Saturday?
   **B** They're going _____ .

# UNIT 6 TIME

## Lesson A Listening

**1** **Complete the words**

1. cl _a_ ss  p _i_ ct _u_ r _e_        4. b ____ b ____
2. f ____ m ____ l ____                  5. p h ____ t ____    ____ l b ____ m
3. g r ____ d ____ ____ t ____ ____ n    6. w ____ d d ____ n g

**2** **Look at the pictures. Write the words from Exercise 1.**

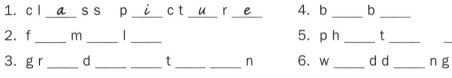

1. Our children's _photo album_

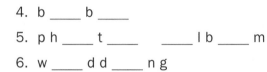

2. Jim and Justin at their high school
   _____ – 6/5/04

3. Our _____
   – 11/94

4. Jim and Deb's _____
   day – 5/9/10

5. Jim and Justin's _____
   _____ – June '92

6. Jim and Deb's _____
   boy, Carl! – 12/11/14

## 3 Look at the pictures in Exercise 2. Circle the correct answers.

1. Jim and Justin became friends _____ .
   a. in school  *(circled)*
   b. in the hospital
   c. at work

2. They graduated from high school on _____ .
   a. May 5, 2004
   b. May 6, 2004
   c. June 5, 2004

3. Jim and Deb got married in _____ .
   a. 1992
   b. 2010
   c. 2007

4. Jim and Deb had a baby on _____ .
   a. December 7, 2011
   b. November 12, 2014
   c. December 11, 2014

5. Jim has _____ .
   a. no brothers or sisters
   b. one sister
   c. one sister and one brother

## 4 Listen. Circle T (True) or F (False).

**Conversation A**

1. Hee and Sue are looking at wedding pictures.    (T)    F
2. Hee got married in 1991.    T    F
3. Sue got married in 1993.    T    F

**Conversation B**

4. Hee and her husband got married in Los Angeles.    T    F
5. Hee moved to Los Angeles in 1996.    T    F
6. Hee's son was born in Los Angeles.    T    F

**Conversation C**

7. Hana started high school last year.    T    F
8. Min graduated from high school in 2012.    T    F
9. Min started college in 2011.    T    F

Check your answers. See page 136.

# Lesson B  When did you move here?

Study the chart on page 128.

**1  Write the verbs in the past tense.**

1. move ___moved___
2. have _____
3. begin _____
4. study _____
5. find _____

6. start _____
7. get _____
8. leave _____
9. meet _____
10. graduate _____

**2  Complete the chart. Use the past tense forms from Exercise 1.**

| Regular verbs (-ed verbs) | Irregular verbs (not -ed verbs) |
| --- | --- |
| moved | had |
| | |
| | |
| | |
| | |

**3  Listen and answer the questions. Use the words in parentheses.**

1. When did you move here?

   (in 2010) _I moved here in 2010._

2. When did Ken start college?

   (in September) _____

3. When did you and your husband meet?

   (in 1998) _____

4. When did you get married?

   (in 2000) _____

5. When did your children begin taking English classes?

   (last year) _____

6. When did Norma leave for vacation?

   (on Saturday) _____

**4** **Read Elsa's time line. Write the questions or answers. Then listen.**

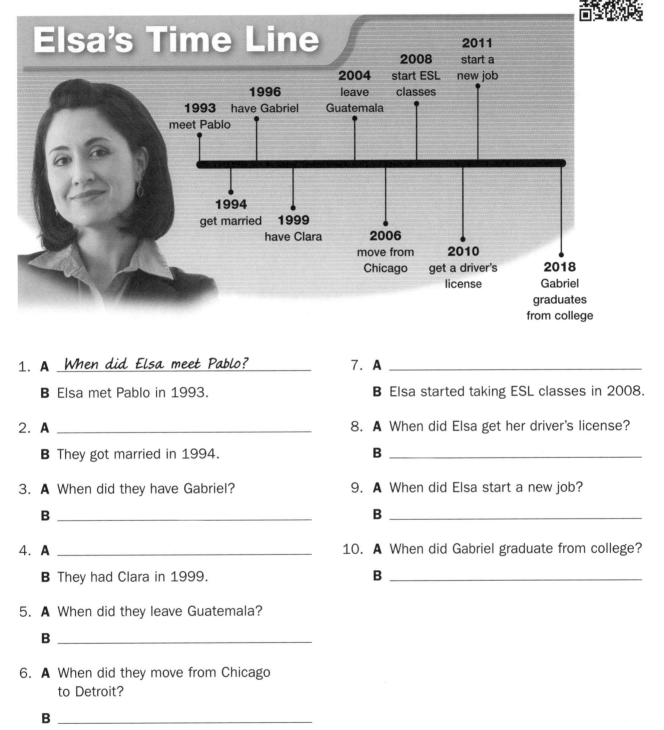

# Elsa's Time Line

**1993** meet Pablo

**1996** have Gabriel

**2004** leave Guatemala

**2008** start ESL classes

**2011** start a new job

**1994** get married

**1999** have Clara

**2006** move from Chicago

**2010** get a driver's license

**2018** Gabriel graduates from college

1. **A** *When did Elsa meet Pablo?*

   **B** Elsa met Pablo in 1993.

2. **A** _____

   **B** They got married in 1994.

3. **A** When did they have Gabriel?

   **B** _____

4. **A** _____

   **B** They had Clara in 1999.

5. **A** When did they leave Guatemala?

   **B** _____

6. **A** When did they move from Chicago to Detroit?

   **B** _____

7. **A** _____

   **B** Elsa started taking ESL classes in 2008.

8. **A** When did Elsa get her driver's license?

   **B** _____

9. **A** When did Elsa start a new job?

   **B** _____

10. **A** When did Gabriel graduate from college?

    **B** _____

# Lesson C  He graduated two years ago.

## 1 Complete the chart for events in the past.

| 1999 | a week | July | noon | the morning |
|---|---|---|---|---|
| 6:15 | December | March 23rd | Saturday | two years |
| a month | four days | May 9th | six months | Wednesday |
| April 11th, 1990 | half past four | night | the afternoon | |

| ago | in | on | at |
|---|---|---|---|
| | *the afternoon* | | |
| | | | |
| | | | |
| | | | |

## 2 Circle the answers.

1. Jeff and Marlena got married **ago** / (**last**) Saturday.

2. Their wedding was **in** / **on** February 1st.

3. The wedding was **at** / **this** noon.

4. They started planning the wedding eight months **ago** / **last**.

5. Marlena found her dress **in** / **on** December.

6. They left for their honeymoon **on** / **this** morning.

7. They need to return **before** / **on** Jeff's new job begins.

8. His new job begins **in** / **on** Monday, February 10th.

9. He quit his old job just **before** / **last** they got married.

10. Marlena started her job three months **after** / **ago**.

**3** **Read Walter's calendar. Today is May 23rd. Complete the sentences. Use *in*, *on*, *at*, *ago*, *last*, *before*, or *after*.**

| May | | | | | | |
|---|---|---|---|---|---|---|
| **Sunday** | **Monday** | **Tuesday** | **Wednesday** | **Thursday** | **Friday** | **Saturday** |
| ~~10~~ shop for my sister's graduation present | ~~11~~ begin new job - 8:00 a.m. | ~~12~~ fix my car after work | ~~13~~ study for citizenship exam | ~~14~~ take citizenship exam - 1:15 | ~~15~~ basketball game - 7:30 p.m. | ~~16~~ Carina's graduation - 2:00 / dinner with family - 6:30 |
| ~~17~~ | ~~18~~ | ~~19~~ take driving test for license - 8:00 a.m. | ~~20~~ doctor's appointment - 4:30 | ~~21~~ take books back to library | ~~22~~ lunch with Carina and her boyfriend | 23 lunch with Mario - noon |

1. Walter had dinner with his sister Carina and her boyfriend _____*last*_____ night.

2. He took his citizenship exam _____ Thursday, May 14th.

3. The test started _____ 1:15.

4. Walter fixed his car two days _____ he took the citizenship exam.

5. He fixed the car _____ the evening.

6. Carina's graduation was a week _____.

7. The family had dinner together _____ Carina's graduation.

8. Walter began his new job _____ week.

**4** **Answer the questions. Use the words in parentheses and the calendar in Exercise 3.**

1. When did Walter take his driving test?
   (ago) *He took his driving test four days ago.*

2. When did Walter shop for his sister's graduation present?
   (last week) _____

3. When did Walter play basketball?
   (Friday, May 15th) _____

4. When did Walter have a doctor's appointment?
   (4:30) _____

5. When did Walter take his books back to the library?
   (ago) _____

**1** **Read and write the correct past tense. Then listen.**

---

## P.C.

Alma ___immigrated___ to the United States ten years ago. In Chile, Alma
       1. immigrate

_____ with computers. Alma _____ English classes after she
  2. work                          3. start

came to the United States.  Alma _____ English for three years. Then,
                           4. study

Alma _____ computer classes. Alma _____ a wonderful man
     5. begin                        6. meet

named Elmer in her computer class. Alma and Elmer _____ in love.
                                           7. fall

After three months, they _____ engaged. They _____ married
                  8. get                  9. get

three years ago. After they got married, they _____ good jobs in a
                             10. find

small computer company. One year later, they got promoted. After two years,

they _____ a small computer business called PC Home Repairs. Last
   11. start

month, Alma and Elmer _____ a baby girl. They _____ to
              12. have                  13. decide

name their baby Patricia Catherina. They call her P.C. for short!

---

**2** **Answer the questions. Use the information from Exercise 1.**

1. When did Alma immigrate to the U.S.?

   _She immigrated ten years ago._ _____

2. When did Alma start English classes?

   _____

3. How long did Alma study English?

   _____

4. When did Alma and Elmer get married?

   _____

5. When did Alma and Elmer find jobs?

   _____

**3** **Number the pictures of Alma's life in the correct order. Use the information from Exercise 1.**

a. _____

b. _____

c. _1_

d. _____

e. _____

f. _____

**4** **Complete the sentences. Use the information from Exercise 1.**

| fell in love | got promoted | retire |
| got engaged | had a baby | started a business |
| got married | immigrated | |

1. Ten years ago, Alma ____*immigrated*____ to the U.S.

2. Alma and Elmer met in their computer class. Then they _____.

3. Three years ago, Alma and Elmer _____.

4. Before they got married, Alma and Elmer _____.

5. One year after they got jobs, Alma and Elmer _____.

6. Two years after they got jobs, Alma and Elmer quit and _____.

7. Last month, Alma and Elmer _____. Her name is Patricia Catherina.

8. When Alma and Elmer are 65, they will probably _____.

## Lesson E Writing

**1 Complete the paragraph. Use the simple past.**

| After | have | in | learn | open | take |
|-------|------|-----|-------|------|------|
| find | In | last | on | start | work |

### A Dream Comes True

Hi-sun Shen immigrated from China to the U.S. _____on_____ January 5,
                                                    1.
2009. She _____ a lot of plans. She _____ English classes
                2.                                    3.
_____ February 2009. She _____ English classes for two years.
       4.                                  5.
She also _____ as a server in a Chinese restaurant. _____
                6.                                                    7.
September 2010, she began vocational school. She _____ to be a chef
                                                          8.
in a Chinese restaurant. _____ two years, she graduated from that
                                9.
program. Then, she _____ a job as a chef in a Chinese restaurant.
                          10.
That was in September 2012. She worked there for six years. But Hi-sun had a

dream. Finally, _____ week, Hi-sun _____ her own restaurant.
                      11.                            12.
She calls her restaurant Hi-sun's Dream.

**2 Complete the time line for Hi-sun.**

a. began vocational school          d. started English classes

b. came to the U.S.                 e. worked as a chef

c. graduated from vocational school f. worked as a server

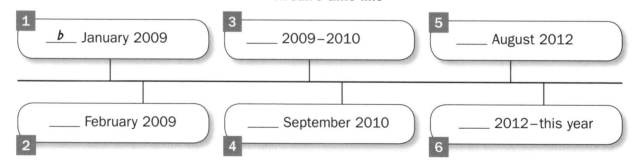

**Hi-sun's time line**

| 1 | __b__ January 2009 | 3 | ____ 2009–2010 | 5 | ____ August 2012 |

| ____ February 2009 | ____ September 2010 | ____ 2012–this year |
| 2 | 4 | 6 |

**3** **Answer the questions. Use the information from Exercises 1 and 2. Write your answers in two different ways.**

1. When did Hi-sun leave China?

   *On January 5, 2009, she left China.*

   *She left China on January 5, 2009.*

2. When did she begin English classes?

   _____

   _____

3. How long did she take English classes?

   _____

   _____

4. When did she begin vocational school?

   _____

   _____

5. In what year did she graduate from vocational school?

   _____

   _____

6. When did she find a job as a chef?

   _____

   _____

7. When did she open her own restaurant?

   _____

   _____

James Johnson
Vocational School

**1** **Read the questions. Look at the school application.**
**Fill in the correct answers.**

**LCC**
**LAGUNA COMMUNITY COLLEGE**

First name _____ *Lin-tao* _____  Middle initial _____ *B* _____  Last name _____ *Ho* _____
Birthdate (Mo/Day/Yr) _____ *9/23/96* _____  Male _____ *X* _____  Female _____
Street address or P.O. box _____ *616 Capstone Street* _____
City _____ *Laguna* _____  State _____ *Washington* _____  Zip code _____ *98103* _____
Email address _____ *compwiz@cup.org* _____  Telephone _____ *206-555-1151* _____
Semester _____ *Fall 2018* _____
Course of study _____ *Computer Technology* _____
Educational goal _____ *2-year certificate* _____
Entry level _____ *First-time student in college* _____
High school education _____ *GED completed 6/12/17* _____
Is your primary language English?  Yes  (No)
If you circled "No": Primary language _____ *Mandarin* _____
What level is your English?
Beginner  Low-intermediate  Intermediate  High-intermediate  (Advanced)
Date of application: _____ *5/23/18* _____

1.  When was Lin-tao born?
    A  9/3/90
    ●  9/23/96
    C  6/12/17
    D  5/23/18

2.  What does Lin-tao want to study?
    A  computer technology
    B  Mandarin
    C  English
    D  GED

3.  When did Lin-tao get his GED?
    A  on June 6, 2017
    B  on June 12, 2017
    C  on December 6, 2017
    D  on May 23, 2017

4.  How long is this course of study?
    A  two years
    B  two semesters
    C  two classes
    D  two weeks

5.  What semester is this application for?
    A  spring
    B  summer
    C  fall
    D  winter

6.  Which statement is true?
    A  Lin-tao was born in the 1980s.
    B  Lin-tao's primary language is English.
    C  Lin-tao didn't finish high school.
    D  Lin-tao's English is very good.

**2** **Look at the chart. Complete the conversations.**
**Use *someone*, *anyone*, *everyone*, or *no one*.**

| | Oscar | Lisa | Rob | Hong |
|---|---|---|---|---|
| 1. Are you married? | | | | |
| 2. Are you single? | ✓ | ✓ | ✓ | ✓ |
| 3. Do you have children? | | | | |
| 4. Do you have a brother? | ✓ | | | |
| 5. Do you have a sister? | | | ✓ | |
| 6. Do you have a middle name? | ✓ | ✓ | ✓ | ✓ |

1. **A** Is _____*anyone*_____ married?

   **B** No, _____*no one*_____ is married.

2. **A** Is _____ single?

   **B** Yes, _____ is single.

3. **A** Does _____ have children?

   **B** No, _____ has children.

4. **A** Does _____ have a brother?

   **B** Yes, _____ has a brother.

5. **A** Does _____ have a sister?

   **B** Yes, _____ has a sister.

6. **A** Does _____ have a middle name?

   **B** Yes, _____ has a middle name.

# UNIT 7 SHOPPING

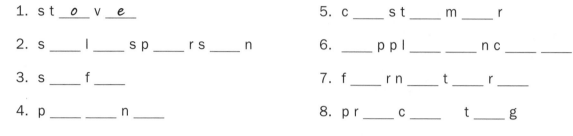

## Lesson A Listening

**1** **Complete the words.**

1. s t __o__ v __e__

2. s ____ l ____ s p ____ r s ____ n

3. s ____ f ____

4. p ____ ____ n ____

5. c ____ s t ____ m ____ r

6. ____ p p l ____ ____ n c ____ ____

7. f ____ r n ____ t ____ r ____

8. p r ____ c ____ ____ t ____ g

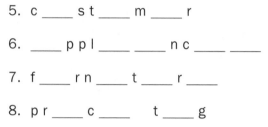

**2** **Look at the pictures. Write the words from Exercise 1.**

1. _____ *sofa* _____

2. _____

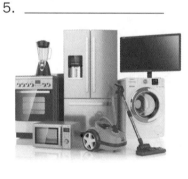

3. _____

4. _____

5. _____

6. _____

7. _____

8. _____

## 3 Listen and complete the conversation.

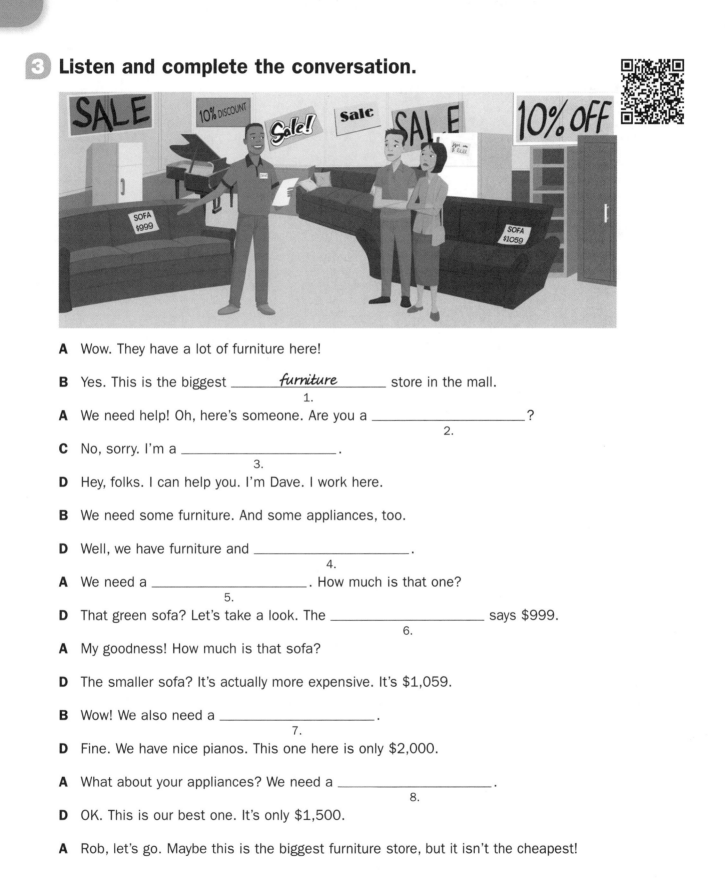

**A** Wow. They have a lot of furniture here!

**B** Yes. This is the biggest _____*furniture*_____ store in the mall.
  1.

**A** We need help! Oh, here's someone. Are you a _____?
  2.

**C** No, sorry. I'm a _____.
  3.

**D** Hey, folks. I can help you. I'm Dave. I work here.

**B** We need some furniture. And some appliances, too.

**D** Well, we have furniture and _____.
  4.

**A** We need a _____. How much is that one?
  5.

**D** That green sofa? Let's take a look. The _____ says $999.
  6.

**A** My goodness! How much is that sofa?

**D** The smaller sofa? It's actually more expensive. It's $1,059.

**B** Wow! We also need a _____.
  7.

**D** Fine. We have nice pianos. This one here is only $2,000.

**A** What about your appliances? We need a _____.
  8.

**D** OK. This is our best one. It's only $1,500.

**A** Rob, let's go. Maybe this is the biggest furniture store, but it isn't the cheapest!

# Lesson B The brown sofa is bigger.

Study the chart on page 131.

## 1 Complete the conversations.

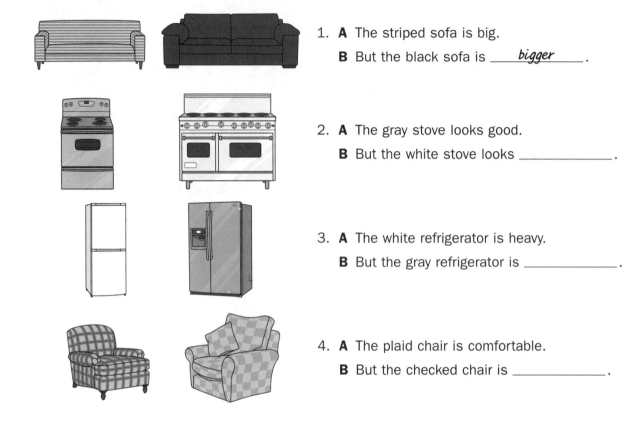

1. **A** The striped sofa is big.
   **B** But the black sofa is ___bigger___.

2. **A** The gray stove looks good.
   **B** But the white stove looks _____.

3. **A** The white refrigerator is heavy.
   **B** But the gray refrigerator is _____.

4. **A** The plaid chair is comfortable.
   **B** But the checked chair is _____.

## 2 Complete the conversation. Use comparatives.

**A** Which chair is ___more comfortable___, the blue chair or the red chair?
                    1. comfortable

**B** I don't know, but the blue chair is _____. I like the pattern and the color.
                                       2. pretty

**A** I do, too. Is it _____?
                  3. expensive

**B** Don't worry about the price. This is a thrift shop! Everything is _____
                                              4. cheap
than in a department store.

**A** Right! Well, the red chair is _____ than the blue chair.
                                  5. big
It's _____, too.
            6. heavy

**B** I want the blue chair.

**A** OK. Let's ask about the price.

**3** **Look at the ad and answer the questions. Then listen.**

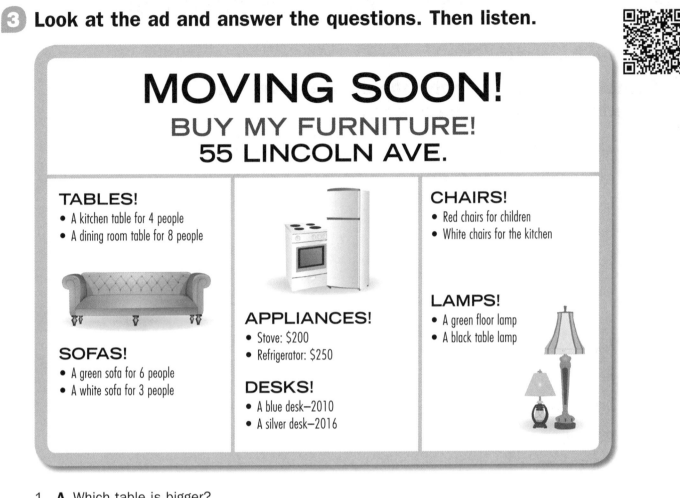

# MOVING SOON!
## BUY MY FURNITURE!
## 55 LINCOLN AVE.

**TABLES!**
- A kitchen table for 4 people
- A dining room table for 8 people

**SOFAS!**
- A green sofa for 6 people
- A white sofa for 3 people

**APPLIANCES!**
- Stove: $200
- Refrigerator: $250

**DESKS!**
- A blue desk—2010
- A silver desk—2016

**CHAIRS!**
- Red chairs for children
- White chairs for the kitchen

**LAMPS!**
- A green floor lamp
- A black table lamp

1. **A** Which table is bigger?

   **B** *The dining room table is bigger.*

2. **A** Which chairs are smaller?

   **B** _____

3. **A** Which appliance is more expensive?

   **B** _____

4. **A** Which desk is older?

   **B** _____

5. **A** Which sofa is longer?

   **B** _____

6. **A** Which lamp is shorter?

   **B** _____

# Lesson C  The yellow chair is the cheapest.

Study the chart on page 131.

**1  Complete the chart. Write the comparative and superlative forms of the adjectives.**

| | Adjective | Comparative | Superlative |
|---|---|---|---|
| 1. | expensive | more expensive | the most expensive |
| 2. | cheap | | |
| 3. | friendly | | |
| 4. | good | | |
| 5. | new | | |
| 6. | heavy | | |
| 7. | low | | |
| 8. | beautiful | | |
| 9. | pretty | | |
| 10. | crowded | | |
| 11. | comfortable | | |
| 12. | nice | | |

**2  Complete the sentences. Use superlatives.**

1. Furniture First has _____the lowest_____ prices of all the furniture stores.
   (low)

2. Robinson's Furniture has _____ chairs.
   (comfortable)

3. Jay Mart's clothes are _____ clothes in the mall.
   (good)

4. Curto's has _____ appliances in town.
   (expensive)

5. Which store has _____ salespeople?
   (nice)

6. Bella's clothes are _____ in the mall.
   (pretty)

7. The furniture at Secondhand Row is _____ in town.
   (cheap)

8. Appliance World is _____ of all the appliance stores.
   (crowded)

9. The SuperPlus TVs are _____ TVs in the store.
   (heavy)

**3** **Complete the chart.**

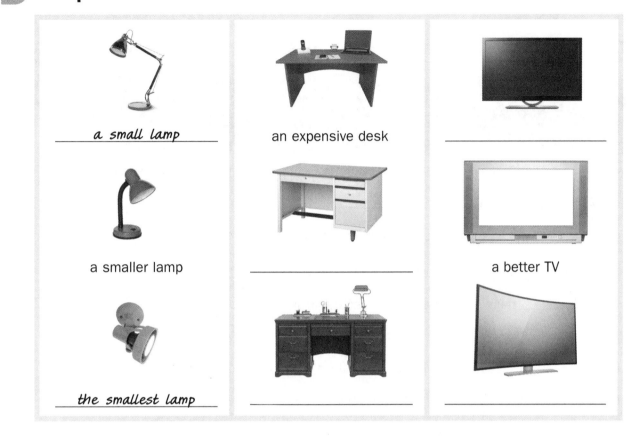

a small lamp

a smaller lamp

the smallest lamp

an expensive desk

a better TV

**4** **Answer the questions.**

## Clothing for Today's Woman

A. jeans skirt $40     B. tennis skirt $55     C. evening skirt $150

1. Which skirt is the most expensive?

   *The evening skirt is the most expensive.*

2. Which skirt is the longest?

3. Which skirt is the cheapest?

4. Which skirt is the shortest?

# Lesson D  Reading

## 1  Read the article. Complete the sentences. Then listen.

### Centerville's Newest Old Store
by Joe Jordan

Antique Alley is the ___newest___ store in Centerville. Antique Alley opened
           1. new

on May 1st, and now it's having a _____ sale. Everything is 50% to 75%
                  2. big

off. Those are the _____ prices for old furniture in Centerville.
           3. good

I visited Antique Alley yesterday. The furniture is _____. For me, the
                  4. beautiful

_____ thing in the store was a large mirror. I didn't buy it because it
    5. nice

was also the _____ thing in the store. It was $1,300! Of course, it was
        6. expensive

also the _____ thing in the store. It was 300 years old. But there were
      7. old

things that were _____ than the mirror. The _____ thing was a
        8. cheap               9. cheap

_____ lamp for only $12.95.
10. small

Visit Antique Alley this weekend. You'll be surprised at what you find.

## 2  Answer the questions.

1. What is the name of the store?

   _The name of the store is Antique Alley._

2. When did it open?

   _____

3. What was the most expensive thing in the store?

   _____

4. Why was it so expensive?

   _____

5. What was the cheapest thing in the store?

   _____

6. Why was it so cheap?

   _____

**3** **Complete the puzzle.**

aquarium    computer desk    entertainment center    mirror    sofa bed
bookcase    end table    furniture    recliner

**Down**

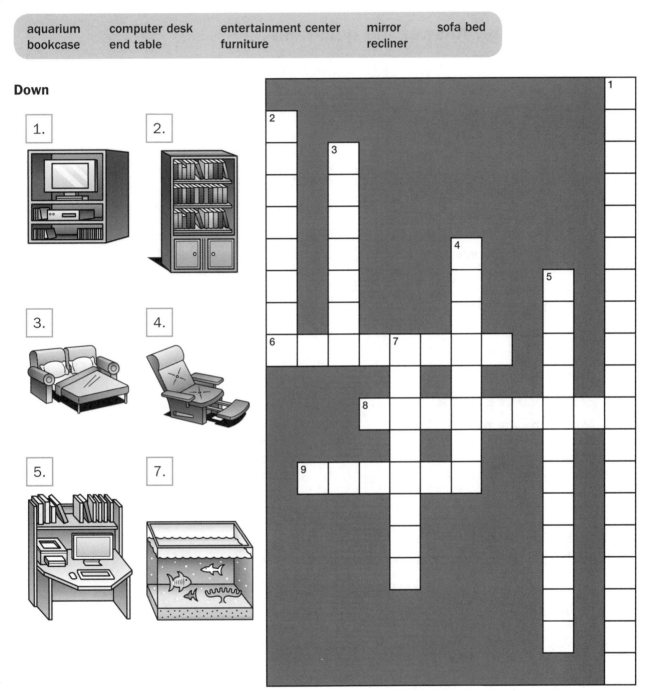

1.    2.

3.    4.

5.    7.

**Across**

6.    8.    9.

# Lesson E Writing

## 1 Read the note. Answer the questions.

Dear Miguel,

This is a special gift because it is your 40th birthday. This is an airline ticket to Mexico. You can visit your brother there. I know you miss him. Happy birthday!

Your loving wife,
Amelia

✈ **Central Airlines**

Departing from:
New York

Going to:
Mexico City

Leave on:
August 10

1. Who is the gift for?

   _The gift is for Miguel._

2. Who is the gift from?

   _____

3. What did she give him?

   _____

4. Why did he receive the gift?

   _____

5. Where will he go?

   _____

6. What day will he leave?

   _____

## 2 Combine the sentences. Use *because*.

1. I bought the red sofa. It was the most comfortable.

   _I bought the red sofa because it was the most comfortable._

2. Sandra gave her sister a pair of earrings. It was her birthday.

   _____

3. Mr. and Mrs. Chung shop at the Clothes Corner. It's the nicest store.

   _____

4. Roberto bought the brown recliner. It was on sale.

   _____

5. I bought an entertainment center. It was 50 percent off.

   _____

**3** **Read the chart. Complete the sentences. Use the comparative or superlative.**

| CENTERVILLE DEPARTMENT STORES | | | | |
|---|---|---|---|---|
| | Opened | Size | Prices | Comments |
| **Best Discounts** | 1983 | 40,000 square feet | very low | nice salespeople |
| Smart Deparment Store | 2013 | 60,000 square feet | very high | beautiful, not crowded |
| Super Discounts | 1970 | 20,000 square feet | medium | crowded |

Yesterday, I needed to buy a lot of things, so I went shopping at Best Discounts. Smart

Department Store is _____*bigger*_____ than Best Discounts, but the salespeople are
                              1. big

_____ at Best Discounts. Also, the prices at Best Discounts are _____
        2. nice                                                                          3. good

than at Smart Department Store. Smart Department Store is _____ than
                                                                      4. new

Best Discounts, and it's also _____ than Best Discounts, but the prices are
                                      5. beautiful

_____.
        6. high

I never go to Super Discounts. It's the _____ department store in town. It's the
                                                  7. old

_____, and it's always the _____.
        8. small                                    9. crowded

**4** **Complete the sentences. Use the chart in Exercise 3. Use the superlative.**

1. (small)      _Super Discounts_   is   _the smallest_   .

2. (old)      _____ is _____.

3. (big)      _____ is _____.

4. (expensive) _____ is _____.

5. (cheap)    _____ is _____.

6. (crowded)  _____ is _____.

## Lesson F Another view

**1** **Read the questions. Look at the ads. Fill in the correct answers.**

**Nick's Nearly New**

Closing Sale. 25-50% off
everything in the store.
**Come and look!**
Used furniture in good condition!
Hours: 9 a.m. to midnight,
7 days a week.
*Deliveries on weekends only.*

**BIG BILL'S BEST FURNITURE**

**FATHER'S DAY SALE!**

All recliners and chairs on sale.
New and used! Only the best.
30-40% discounts.
**FREE DELIVERY.**

Hours:
8:00 a.m. – 6:00 p.m.
Mon. – Sat.

**MODERN FURNITURE**

Everything on sale! 50–80% off. China Cabinets, Bookcases, Beds,
Sofa Beds, Coffee Tables, Entertainment Centers, Kitchen Appliances.
We have it all. It's all new!

HOURS: 11:00 – 9:00 MONDAY THROUGH FRIDAY AND 12:00 – 9:00 ON SATURDAY.
BRING A VAN AND TAKE IT HOME. EXTRA FOR DELIVERY.

1. Which store has only used furniture?
   - (A) Big Bill's
   - (B) Modern Furniture
   - ● Nick's Nearly New
   - (D) all of the above

2. Which store makes deliveries?
   - (A) Big Bill's
   - (B) Modern Furniture
   - (C) Nick's Nearly New
   - (D) all of the above

3. Which store has new and used furniture?
   - (A) Big Bill's
   - (B) Modern Furniture
   - (C) Nick's Nearly New
   - (D) all of the above

4. Which store has a Father's Day Sale?
   - (A) Big Bill's
   - (B) Modern Furniture
   - (C) Nick's Nearly New
   - (D) all of the above

5. Which store is open on Sunday?
   - (A) Big Bill's
   - (B) Modern Furniture
   - (C) Nick's Nearly New
   - (D) all of the above

6. Which statement is true?
   - (A) The biggest discounts are at Big Bill's.
   - (B) Modern Furniture charges extra for delivery.
   - (C) Big Bill's has the best furniture.
   - (D) All of Nick's furniture is new.

**2** **Look at the ad. Complete the sentences. Use *one*, *some*, *the other*, and *the others*.**

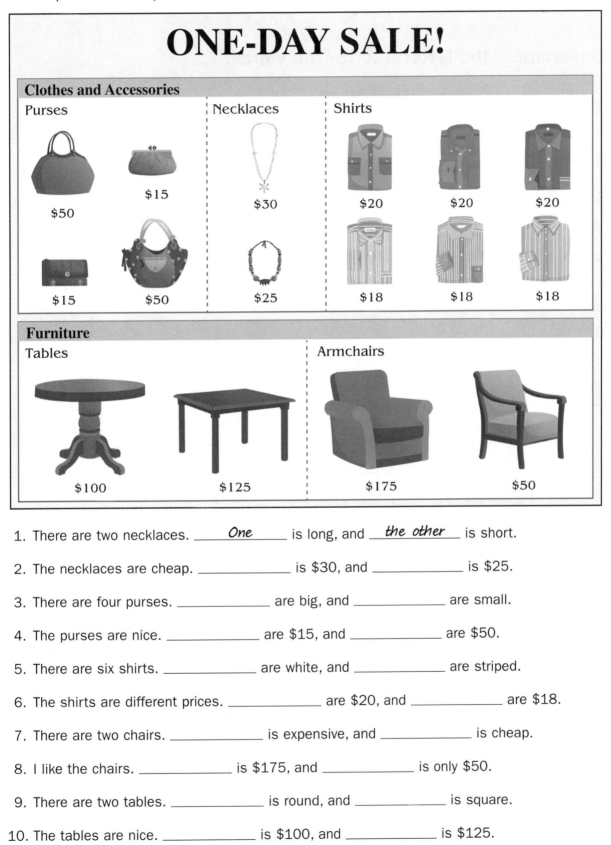

# ONE-DAY SALE!

**Clothes and Accessories**

Purses

$50

$15

$15

$50

Necklaces

$30

$25

Shirts

$20

$20

$20

$18

$18

$18

**Furniture**

Tables

$100

$125

Armchairs

$175

$50

1. There are two necklaces. _____One_____ is long, and __the other__ is short.

2. The necklaces are cheap. _____ is $30, and _____ is $25.

3. There are four purses. _____ are big, and _____ are small.

4. The purses are nice. _____ are $15, and _____ are $50.

5. There are six shirts. _____ are white, and _____ are striped.

6. The shirts are different prices. _____ are $20, and _____ are $18.

7. There are two chairs. _____ is expensive, and _____ is cheap.

8. I like the chairs. _____ is $175, and _____ is only $50.

9. There are two tables. _____ is round, and _____ is square.

10. The tables are nice. _____ is $100, and _____ is $125.

## Lesson A Listening

**1** **Unscramble the letters. Write the words.**

1. bla      _____lab_____

2. derlyor      _____

3. oc-rkerwos      _____

4. kerwal      _____

5. inensl      _____

6. tentiap      _____

7. liessupp      _____

8. hailwhreec      _____

**2** **Look at the picture. Write the words from Exercise 1.**

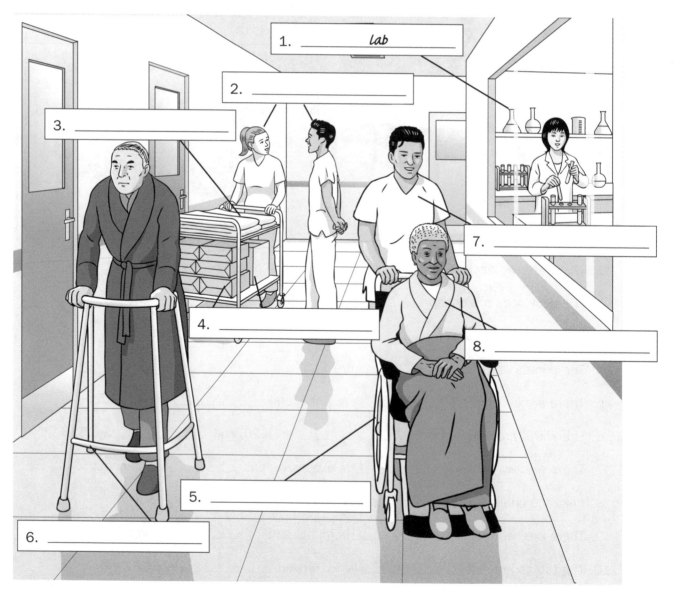

1. _____lab_____
2. _____
3. _____
4. _____
5. _____
6. _____
7. _____
8. _____

## 3 Complete the sentences.

co-workers   linens   orderly   patient   walker   wheelchair

1. The _____patient_____ came to the hospital with a broken leg.

2. Suzanne and her two _____ worked the night shift together.

3. Suzanne put clean _____ on the bed.

4. Because he broke his leg, Sam had to ride in a _____ .

5. The _____ took the X-rays to the lab.

6. Anne is very old. She needs to use a _____ when she walks.

## 4 Listen. Circle T (True) or F (False).

**Conversation A**

| | | |
|---|---|---|
| 1. Otto has a new job. | (T) | F |
| 2. Otto delivered a walker to a patient yesterday. | T | F |
| 3. Otto cleans rooms. | T | F |

**Conversation B**

| | | |
|---|---|---|
| 4. Otto started his job a few months ago. | T | F |
| 5. Otto needs to work full-time now. | T | F |
| 6. Otto wants to be a medical assistant. | T | F |

**Conversation C**

| | | |
|---|---|---|
| 7. Otto is in an office at Valley Hospital. | T | F |
| 8. Otto can go to school part-time and work part-time. | T | F |
| 9. Otto can't take classes at night. | T | F |

## 5 Make the false statements in Exercise 4 true. Write.

_____

_____

_____

_____

_____

# Lesson B  Where did you go last night?

Study the chart on page 128.

## 1  Match the questions with the answers.

1. Where did you go last night? _c_

2. What did you take to the party? _____

3. What did Cristal do after breakfast? _____

4. Where did your parents meet? _____

5. What did they do after they came to the U.S.? _____

6. What did Jon pick up at your house? _____

7. Where did you and Andy go this morning? _____

a. They worked in restaurants.

b. She cleaned the house.

c. I went to the movies.

d. He picked up a uniform.

e. I took a cake to the party.

f. We went to the beach.

g. They met at school.

## 2  Read the answers. Write *What* or *Where*.

1. **A** _____What_____ did you do last night?

   **B** I worked the night shift.

2. **A** _____ did you go after work?

   **B** I went out for breakfast.

3. **A** _____ did Max do after breakfast?

   **B** He took the bus to school.

4. **A** _____ did Sheila do at work this morning?

   **B** She made the beds with new linens.

5. **A** _____ did you and your family eat dinner last night?

   **B** We ate dinner at Tony's Pizzeria.

6. **A** _____ did Sheila and Max do last weekend?

   **B** They went to the park for a picnic.

7. **A** _____ did you do after the concert?

   **B** We went for coffee.

8. **A** _____ did Max go last Sunday?

   **B** He went to the baseball game.

**3** **Read and complete the questions and answers.**
**Use *What* or *Where* and the simple past. Then listen.**

> **Mai**
> • meet new patients in reception area—9:00
> • take the patient in Room 304 to the lab—9:30
> • make the bed in Room 304
> • take patients from lab to their rooms—10:00
> • help nurses on the fourth floor—10:45
> • lunch in the cafeteria—12:30

> **Jorge**
> • meet new patients in reception area—9:00
> • pick up X-rays from lab—9:30
> • deliver X-rays to doctors
> • help patient in Room 310—10:00
> • prepare rooms on the second floor —11:30
> • lunch in the cafeteria—12:30

1. **A** _____What_____ did Mai and Jorge do at 9:00?

   **B** _____

2. **A** _____ did Mai take her patient at 9:30?

   **B** _____

3. **A** _____ did Jorge do at 9:30?

   **B** _____

4. **A** _____ did Mai and Jorge do after 9:30?

   **B** Mai _____, and Jorge _____

5. **A** _____ did Jorge go at 10:00?

   **B** _____

6. **A** _____ did Jorge do in Room 310?

   **B** _____

7. **A** _____ did Mai do at 10:00?

   **B** _____

8. **A** _____ did Mai go after that?

   **B** _____

9. **A** _____ did Jorge do at 11:30?

   **B** _____

# Lesson C I work on Saturdays and Sundays.

## 1 Complete the sentences. Use *and*, *or*, or *but*.

1. Mateo has two jobs. He works in a restaurant _____*and*_____ in an office.

2. We can have lunch at Sub's _____ at Carl's.

3. Gu-jan talked to his mother about his job plans, _____ he didn't talk to his father.

4. After work, Lourdes had cake _____ ice cream.

5. Mandy and Paco went to New York, _____ they didn't see the Statue of Liberty.

6. Ivan works the day shift _____ the night shift. He never works both shifts.

7. Sally works at the hospital during the week _____ at Pizza Town on the weekend.

8. At work, Ang answers the phones _____ takes messages.

## 2 Combine the sentences. Use *and*, *or*, or *but*.

1. Sometimes Jun eats lunch at noon. Sometimes Jun eats lunch at 1:00.
   *Jun eats lunch at noon or at 1:00.*

2. Javier helps the nurses. He also helps the doctors.
   _____

3. Tien picks up the supplies at the warehouse. She doesn't deliver the supplies.
   _____

4. Rieko met her new co-workers this morning. She didn't meet any patients.
   _____

5. At the restaurant, Mustafa made the soup. He also made the salad.
   _____

6. Sometimes Anatoly drinks coffee. Sometimes he drinks tea.
   _____

**3** **Read the chart. Write sentences. Use *and* or *but* and the simple past.**

| Office Assistant Duties – Friday 11/29 | | |
|---|---|---|
| Rachel | Dora | Adam |
| Prepare the meeting room<br>Pick up supplies<br>Deliver the mail | Make the coffee<br>Go to the meeting<br>Answer calls<br>Take messages | Check the office email<br>Go to the meeting<br>Take notes<br>Make copies |

1. Dora / go to the meeting / take notes

   *Dora went to the meeting, but she didn't take notes.*

2. Adam / check the office email / go to the meeting

   _____

3. Rachel / prepare the meeting room / make the coffee

   _____

4. Dora and Adam / go to the meeting / prepare the meeting room

   _____

5. Adam / take notes / make copies

   _____

6. Rachel / pick up supplies / deliver the mail

   _____

**4** **Complete the sentences with *and*, *or*, or *but*.**

| | Monday | Tuesday | Wednesday | Thursday | Friday |
|---|---|---|---|---|---|
| This week | Rachel | Dora | Adam | Dora | Adam |
| Next week | Adam | Dora | Rachel | Dora | Adam |

Please eat lunch at your desk and answer calls on these days:

1. Dora eats lunch at her desk on Tuesday _____*and*_____ Thursday.

2. On Monday, Rachel _____ Adam answer calls.

3. This week, Adam eats lunch at his desk on Wednesday _____ Friday.

4. Dora and Adam eat lunch at their desks twice a week, _____ Rachel doesn't. She eats lunch at her desk only once a week.

**1** **Read and circle the correct answers. Then listen.**

| | |
|---|---|
| To: | personnel@newtownmedical.com |
| From: | cmcintosh@wcc.org |
| Date: | May 25, 2018 |
| Subject: | Federico Robles |

To Whom It May Concern:

I am happy to write this recommendation for Federico Robles. Federico is a student in the Medical Assistant Certificate Program here at WCC. He will graduate in June.

Federico is an excellent student and a hard worker. He can manage a medical office, schedule appointments, and take care of patient records. He can assist doctors with many duties.

I recommend Federico very highly. He will be an excellent medical assistant. Please contact me for more information.

Sincerely,

Carrie McIntosh

Instructor  **WCC** | WESTPORT COMMUNITY COLLEGE

1. Carrie McIntosh is Federico's _____.
   a. boss
   b. medical assistant
   c. instructor

2. This recommendation is about _____.
   a. Carrie McIntosh
   b. Federico
   c. Federico's new boss

3. Federico can _____.
   a. manage a medical office
   b. schedule appointments
   c. both a and b

4. Federico _____.
   a. is looking for a job
   b. is going to start school
   c. has a job now

5. In June, Federico is going to _____.
   a. get a new job
   b. graduate
   c. quit his job

6. What is the purpose of this email?
   a. to say hello to Federico
   b. to help Federico get a job
   c. to find a new medical assistant

**2** **Answer the questions.**

1. Who wrote the email? _Carrie McIntosh wrote the email._

2. When did she write the email? _____

3. Where does she teach? _____

4. What program does she teach in? _____

5. What job skills did Federico learn? List them. _____

_____

## 3 Match the jobs with the pictures.

**a.**

**b.**

**c.**

**d.**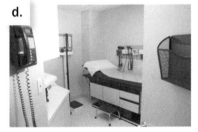

1. auto mechanic

2. orderly

3. homemaker

4. cashier

5. construction worker

6. medical assistant

7. cook

8. teacher

**e.**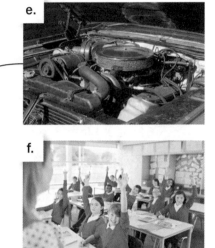

**f.**

**g.**

**h.**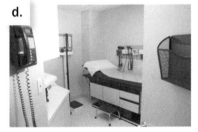

## 4 Complete the sentences. Use the jobs from Exercise 3.

1. A _____*homemaker*_____ takes care of a family.

2. A _____ operates large machines.

3. An _____ helps the nurses.

4. A _____ assists the doctor.

5. An _____ repairs cars.

6. A _____ teaches students.

7. A _____ handles money.

8. A _____ prepares food.

# Lesson E Writing

**1** **Read Michael's employment history. Complete the sentences. Use the correct form of the verb.**

**Employment History: Michael Bitter**

Michael Bitter is a medical assistant. He _____ at Valley Medical Clinic. He started
                                        1. work
in 2017. He _____ appointments for patients. He _____ the phones and
              2. make                                        3. answer
_____ messages. He _____ the patients and _____ the doctors.
4. take                        5. prepare                        6. assist
    From 2003 to 2015, Michael _____ at Freshie's Pizza. He had two jobs there.
                                  7. work
From 2011 to 2015, he _____ a cashier. He _____ money and _____
                          8. be                        9. handle                    10. operate
the credit card machine. From 2003 to 2011, he _____ a busperson.
                                                  11. be
    Michael _____ to Westport Community College from 2015 to 2017. He
              12. go
_____ a full-time student in the Medical Assistant Certificate Program. He _____
13. be                                                                                  14. graduate
in June 2017. In June 2012, he _____ his GED at Staples Adult School.
                                  15. get

**2** **Answer the questions. Use the employment history in Exercise 1.**

1. When did Michael start his job at the medical clinic?

   *He started his job at the medical clinic in 2017.*

2. Where did he work for 12 years?

   _____

3. What did he do from 2015 to 2017?

   _____

4. Where did he study for his GED?

   _____

5. When did he get his GED?

   _____

6. Where does he work now?

   _____

## 3 Rewrite the sentences. Use the simple past.

1. I prepare food, but I don't clear the tables.

   *I prepared food, but I didn't clear the tables.*

2. I handle money and talk to people every day.

   _____

3. I help the nurses, but I don't help the doctors.

   _____

4. I take care of my children and my house.

   _____

5. I clear tables and handle money, but I don't prepare food.

   _____

6. I operate large machines and build houses.

   _____

## 4 Match the pictures with the sentences in Exercise 3. Then write the words.

| | | |
|---|---|---|
| busperson | construction worker | homemaker |
| cashier | cook | orderly |

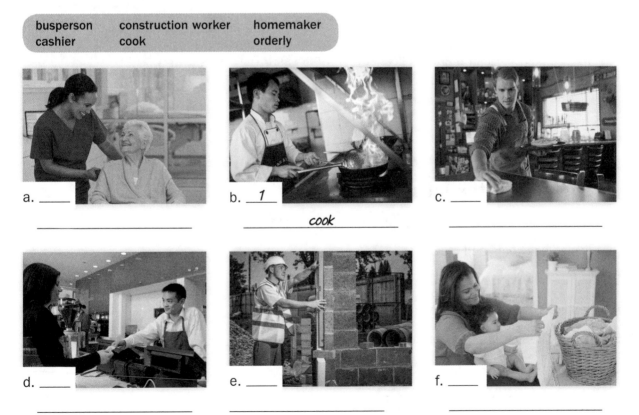

a. ____
_____

b. _1_
_____ *cook* _____

c. ____
_____

d. ____
_____

e. ____
_____

f. ____
_____

# Lesson F Another view

**1** **Read the job ads. Write the words. Start each word with a capital letter.**

auto mechanic    busperson    cashier    construction worker    medical assistant    orderly

1. _____Orderly_____ Needed.
Help patients walk, take patients for X-rays, deliver X-rays and mail, help nurses, talk to patients. No experience necessary.

4. _____ Wanted.
Medical office needs friendly worker. Assist doctor and take care of office. Experience or Medical Assistant Certificate needed.

2. _____ Wanted.
You will need to handle money, use a cash register, know basic math, be friendly with customers, and be on time. Restaurant experience necessary.

5. _____ Needed.
Busy car repair shop needs worker. Experience with American and foreign cars useful. Five years of experience necessary.

3. _____ Needed.
You need to have two years of experience building houses. Need a driver's license. Need to be able to work alone.

6. _____ Wanted.
New restaurant needs worker to clear and clean tables. No experience necessary. Need to work fast.

**2** **Read the sentences. Which job is best for each person? Write the jobs from Exercise 1.**

1. I am friendly and like to help people.     _____orderly_____

2. I like to use tools and machines.          _____

3. I can handle money, and I like math.       _____

4. I repaired cars for seven years.           _____

5. I cleared tables in a restaurant last year. _____

6. I like to work alone.                      _____

7. I have a Medical Assistant Certificate.    _____

8. I can work fast.                           _____

**3** **Look at the chart. Write sentences about Dani.**
**Use *can*, *can't*, *could*, and *couldn't*.**

|  | Ten years ago | Now |
|---|---|---|
| cook | No | Yes |
| dance | Yes | No |
| drive | No | No |
| run fast | Yes | No |
| play the piano | Yes | Yes |
| read English | No | Yes |
| speak Spanish | No | Yes |
| take care of a family | No | Yes |

1. Dani ____*couldn't*____ cook ten years ago, but she _____*can*_____ cook now.

2. Dani _____ dance ten years ago, but she _____ dance now.

3. Dani _____ drive ten years ago, and she _____ drive now.

4. Dani _____ run fast ten years ago, but she _____ run fast now.

5. Dani _____ play the piano ten years ago, and she _____ play the piano now.

6. Dani _____ read English ten years ago, but she _____ read English now.

7. Dani _____ speak Spanish ten years ago, but she _____ speak Spanish now.

8. Dani _____ take care of a family ten years ago, but she _____ take care of a family now.

# UNIT 9 DAILY LIVING

## Lesson A Listening

**1** **Look at the picture. Write the words.**

| | | | |
|---|---|---|---|
| dishwasher | garbage | lightbulb | sink |
| dryer | leak | lock | washing machine |

1. _____lightbulb_____

2. _____

3. _____

4. _____

5. _____

6. _____

7. _____

8. _____

Jack    Juliana    Jenny

**2** **Complete the sentences. Use the words from Exercise 1.**

1. Jenny is taking out the _____garbage_____.

2. She is unlocking the door. Her hand is on the _____.

3. Juliana is changing a _____.

4. Jack is washing the dishes in the _____.

5. There is water on the floor in front of the _____.

6. The dishwasher has a _____.

7. There is soapy water coming from the _____.

8. There are clothes on top of the _____.

**3** Look at the picture in Exercise 1. Answer the questions.

1. How many appliances does Juliana have in her kitchen?
   *She has five appliances in her kitchen.*

2. Which appliances does she have?
   _____

3. How many appliances have problems?
   _____

4. Which appliances have problems?
   _____

**4** Listen. Circle the correct answers.

**Conversation A**

1. Who is Steve calling?
   a. a neighbor
   b. the building manager
   c. a plumber

2. Steve has a problem with _____.
   a. the sink and the dishwasher
   b. the washing machine and the dishwasher
   c. the washing machine and the sink

3. The better plumber is _____.
   a. the Brown Plumbing Company
   b. the Green Company
   c. Gemelli Plumbers

**Conversation B**

4. Who is Linda?
   a. a neighbor
   b. a receptionist
   c. a building manager

5. Steve lives on _____.
   a. 15th Street
   b. Second Avenue
   c. Fourth Street

6. Mark can come _____.
   a. at 9:00
   b. at noon
   c. at 4:00

**Conversation C**

7. Who is Steve calling?
   a. a neighbor
   b. a plumber
   c. the building manager

8. When did Ms. Ling's sink overflow?
   a. last month
   b. last week
   c. this morning

9. When will Ms. Ling be back?
   a. at 9:00
   b. at 10:00
   c. at 11:00

# Lesson B  Can you call a plumber, please?

**1** **Rewrite the questions. Use the words in parentheses.**

1. Can you call a plumber, please?

   (Could) _Could you call a plumber, please?_

2. Could you fix the window, please?

   (Would) _____

3. Would you fix the lock, please?

   (Will) _____

4. Could you fix the dryer, please?

   (Would) _____

5. Would you unclog the sink, please?

   (Could) _____

6. Would you repair the oven, please?

   (Can) _____

**2** **Circle the correct answers.**

1. Could you fix the window?
   a. No, I'd be happy to.
   b. Yes, of course.

2. Would you repair the dishwasher?
   a. Sorry, I can't right now.
   b. Sorry, I'd be happy to.

3. Can you unclog the sink?
   a. No, of course.
   b. Yes, I'd be happy to.

4. Will you fix the lock now, please?
   a. No, not now. Maybe later.
   b. No, I'd be happy to.

5. Could you call an electrician now, please?
   a. Sure. Maybe later.
   b. Yes, of course.

6. Would you repair the toilet now, please?
   a. No, I can right now.
   b. Sorry, I can't right now.

**3** **Look at the picture. Make requests for the landlord.**

1. **A** _Could you fix the window, please?_
   (Could / fix / window)
   **B** Sure, I'd be happy to.

2. **A** _____
   (Would / repair / refrigerator)
   **B** No, not now. Maybe later.

3. **A** _____
   (Can / fix / light)
   **B** Yes, of course.

4. **A** _____
   (Will / unclog / sink)
   **B** Sorry, I can't right now.

5. **A** _____
   (Could / repair / lock)
   **B** No, not now. Maybe later.

6. **A** _____
   (Would / fix / dishwasher)
   **B** Yes, of course. I'd be happy to.

**4** **Read the list. Listen and make requests with _Could_.**

1. **A** _Could you fix the light, please?_
   **B** No, maybe later.

2. **A** _____
   **B** Yes, of course.

3. **A** _____
   **B** Sorry, I can't right now.

4. **A** _____
   **B** Sure. I'd be happy to.

5. **A** _____
   **B** Yes, of course.

6. **A** _____
   **B** No, maybe later.

1. ~~fix the light~~
2. unclog the bathtub
3. change the lightbulb
4. repair the dishwasher
5. clean the carpet
6. call a plumber

# Lesson C  Which one do you recommend?

Study the chart on page 127.

## 1 Complete each question with *do* or *does*. Then write the answer.

1. Which plumber _____*do*_____ they recommend?
   (Jerry's Plumbing) _They recommend Jerry's Plumbing._

2. Which teacher _____ he recommend?
   (Joe Thompson) _____

3. Which electrician _____ you recommend?
   (Wired Electric) _____

4. Which pharmacy _____ they recommend?
   (Rite Price) _____

5. Which bank _____ she recommend?
   (Bank and Trust) _____

6. Which supermarket _____ he recommend?
   (SaveMore) _____

## 2 Answer the questions. Use the words in parentheses.

1. Which babysitter does Marian recommend?
   (her cousin) _Marian recommends her cousin._

2. Which plumber do you suggest?
   (Drains R Us) _____

3. Which auto mechanic does your husband like?
   (Ed Peterson) _____

4. Which doctor does your daughter recommend?
   (Dr. White) _____

5. Which supermarket do you and your family like?
   (Food City) _____

6. Which ESL program does your wife recommend?
   (Rockland Adult School)

   _____

7. Which clinic do you and your husband suggest?
   (the City Clinic) _____

## 3 Read the ads. Circle the answers.

1. It's Saturday, and your friend's dishwasher has a leak.

   You recommend **Fix It** / **(ABC.)**

2. You want a licensed repair person to fix your dryer.

   Your friend recommends **Fix It** / **ABC**.

3. Your mother needs a repair person for her stove right now.

   You recommend **Fix It** / **ABC**.

4. You want the repair person to clean the floor after the job is finished.

   Your parents recommend **Fix It** / **ABC**.

## 4 Read the ads. Write the answers. Give reasons.

1. Which locksmith do you recommend?

   (All Keys / 24 hours) _I recommend All Keys because it's open 24 hours._

2. Which locksmith do they suggest?

   (Smitty's / licensed) _____

3. Which locksmith does Harry like?

   (All Keys / more experienced) _____

4. Which locksmith does Muriel suggest?

   (Smitty's / free keys) _____

5. Which locksmith do the Corwins recommend?

   (All Keys / fast service) _____

# Lesson D Reading

## 1 Read and circle the correct answers. Then listen.

---

From: Rico Martinez <rmar14@cup.org>

To: Jenna and Enrique Martinez <jem45@cup.org>

Date: January 8, 2018

Subject: New Apartment

---

How are you? We're all fine. We moved into our new apartment one week ago. It's very nice. There are some problems, but our landlord will fix them. There are two big bedrooms – one for the children and one for us. The carpet in the children's bedroom is stained, but the landlord is going to put in a new carpet tomorrow. Also, the curtains in our bedroom are torn. Claudia is going to make new curtains for all the rooms. She bought some beautiful material on sale. Some of the windows are jammed, but they are very big. It's winter now, and we don't need to open them. The landlord will fix them before spring. It's a really nice apartment. The rooms are big and sunny. Come and visit us soon!

---

1. What is the landlord going to do tomorrow?
   a. fix the windows
   b. put in a new carpet
   c. repair the curtains

2. What is Claudia going to do?
   a. fix the curtains
   b. make new curtains
   c. wash the curtains

3. Rico is not upset about the jammed windows. Why?
   a. because it's cold outside
   b. because it's hot outside
   c. because the landlord will fix them tomorrow

4. What is the problem in the children's bedroom?
   a. The windows are broken.
   b. The curtains are torn.
   c. The carpet is stained.

5. What does Rico like about the apartment?
   a. It's sunny and the rooms are big.
   b. The landlord is nice.
   c. The curtains are beautiful.

6. Why did Rico write this email?
   a. to complain about his landlord
   b. to tell his parents about his new apartment
   c. to make plans for the spring

## 2 Look at the picture. Write the words.

| | | |
|---|---|---|
| bent | cracked | scratched |
| broken | dripping | stained |
| burned out | jammed | torn |

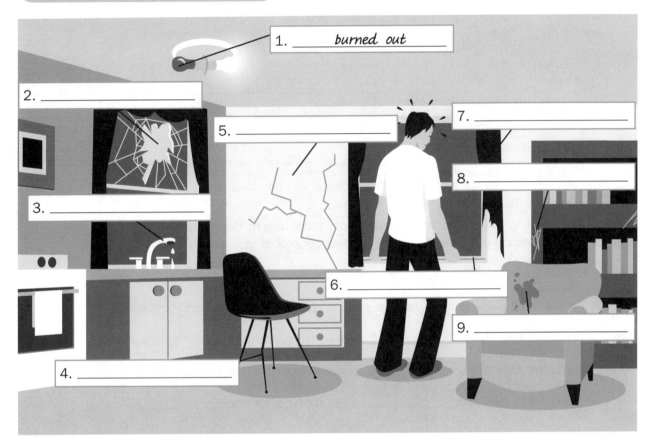

1. _____burned out_____

2. _____

7. _____

5. _____

8. _____

3. _____

6. _____

9. _____

4. _____

## 3 Complete the sentences. Use words from Exercise 2.

1. One window won't open. It's _____*jammed*_____.

2. The other window is _____.

3. One lightbulb is _____.

4. The faucet in the kitchen is _____.

5. The curtain is _____.

6. The wall is _____.

7. One chair has a _____ leg.

8. The other chair is _____.

9. The bookcase is _____.

# Lesson E Writing

## 1 Read the email. Write the words.

broken      clogged      dripping      scratched
burned out  cracked      jammed        stained

From: Jim Bowen (jbowen@ micro.com)

To: Ms. Torrant (atorrant@rsl.net)

Date: December 2, 2017

Subject: Apartment Problems

Dear Ms. Torrant,

I am writing on behalf of myself and several other tenants in your apartment building. We are contacting you because we are upset about problems in the building.

There are ____broken____ windows and many _____ ceilings. You need
               1.                     2.

to paint the walls because they are _____. We can't open some windows
                                3.

because they are _____. You need to replace many of the lightbulbs in the
                   4.

halls because they are _____. Some faucets in the sinks are _____.
                   5.                          6.

Also, many doors are _____, and some toilets are _____.
                 7.                     8.

Please reply to Jim Bowen in Apartment 822. Thank you for your attention.

Jim Bowen, Apt. 822

Sharmin Patel, Apt. 201

Randy Jones, Apt. 412

Brad Wilson, Apt. 605

## 2 Answer the questions. Use the information from Exercise 1.

1. Who sent the email? _Jim Bowen_ _____

2. List all the apartment numbers in the email. _____

3. What is the subject line of this email? _____

4. Who is the email written to? _____

5. How many people are upset? _____

6. Who should Ms. Torrant reply to? _____

**3** **Read the list of problems. Complete the email.**

---

**List of Problems for:**
**78 Hillspoint Road Apartments**

| Apartment | Problem |
|---|---|
| 4B | Leaking dishwasher |
| 6A | Stained carpet |
| 1B | Cracked bathtub |
| 2C | Clogged toilet |
| 3A | Broken stove |

---

○ ○ ○

From: cvaldez1@atlas.com

To: treelake45@web.net

Date: July 2, 2018

Subject: Apartment Problems

Dear Mr. Treelake,

I am a tenant in your apartment building at 78 Hillspoint Road. I am writing to you about some problems in the apartments.

Apartment 1B has a _cracked bathtub_ . The _____ in Apartment 4B is
                  1.                            2.

_____ . The tenants in Apartment 2C have a _____ . Could
      3.                                     4.

you please call a plumber to fix these three problems?

Also, the _____ in Apartment 3A is _____ . The tenants
           5.                              6.

can't use it. Would you please call a repair person?

The _____ in Apartment 6A is _____ . You need to clean it.
        7.                                8.

You need to fix these problems right away. Your tenants are upset. Please call me at (825) 555-1574. Thank you for your attention.

Sincerely,

Claire Valdez

Apartment 5C

**1** **Read the questions. Look at the invoice. Fill in the correct answers.**

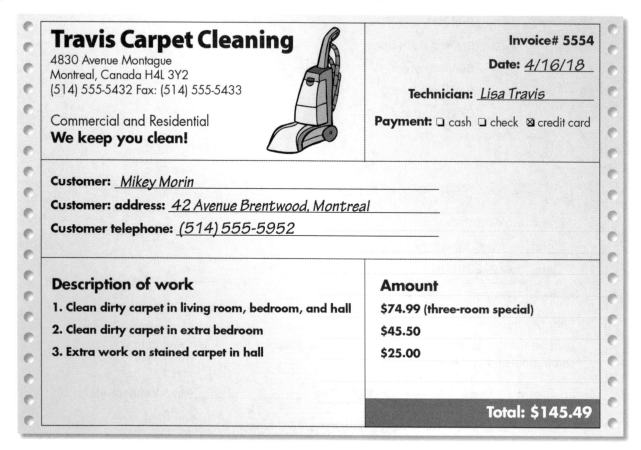

**Travis Carpet Cleaning**
4830 Avenue Montague
Montreal, Canada H4L 3Y2
(514) 555-5432 Fax: (514) 555-5433

Commercial and Residential
**We keep you clean!**

Invoice# 5554

**Date:** _4/16/18_

**Technician:** _Lisa Travis_

**Payment:** ☐ cash  ☐ check  ☒ credit card

**Customer:** _Mikey Morin_

**Customer: address:** _42 Avenue Brentwood, Montreal_

**Customer telephone:** _(514) 555-5952_

| Description of work | Amount |
| --- | --- |
| 1. Clean dirty carpet in living room, bedroom, and hall | $74.99 (three-room special) |
| 2. Clean dirty carpet in extra bedroom | $45.50 |
| 3. Extra work on stained carpet in hall | $25.00 |

**Total: $145.49**

1. How much was the three-room special?
   - (A) $25.00
   - (B) $45.50
   - (●) $74.99
   - (D) $145.49

2. Where was the stained carpet?
   - (A) in the hall
   - (B) in the bedroom
   - (C) in the extra bedroom
   - (D) in the living room

3. How much is the total?
   - (A) $25.00
   - (B) $45.50
   - (C) $74.99
   - (D) $145.49

4. Who is the customer?
   - (A) Lisa Travis
   - (B) Mikey Morin
   - (C) Montague
   - (D) Travis Carpet Cleaning

5. How did the customer pay?
   - (A) with cash
   - (B) by check
   - (C) by credit card
   - (D) none of the above

6. Which carpet cleaning was the most expensive?
   - (A) the living room
   - (B) the extra bedroom
   - (C) the bedroom
   - (D) the hall

**2** **Complete the conversation about the new apartment.**
**Use *let's* and *let's not* with *buy*, *make*, *fix*, or *clean*.**

1. **A** The window is broken.

   **B** _____*Let's fix*_____ it.

   **A** OK, _____*let's fix*_____ it.

2. **A** The couch is stained.

   **B** I know. _____ a new couch.

   **A** No, _____ a new one. It's too expensive. _____
   it ourselves. I have a special cleaner for couch material.

3. **A** The curtains are torn.

   **B** _____ new curtains.

   **A** No, _____ new curtains. _____ new curtains.
   I have some beautiful material.

4. **A** That chair has a broken leg.

   **B** Yes. _____ a new chair.

   **A** OK. _____ two new chairs!

5. **A** The carpet is stained.

   **B** I know. _____ it ourselves.

   **A** Good idea. _____ some carpet cleaner.

# UNIT 10 FREE TIME

**1** **Look at the picture. Write the words.**

| a cake | a guest | a present | flowers |
|--------|---------|-----------|---------|
| a card | a piece of cake | balloons | perfume |

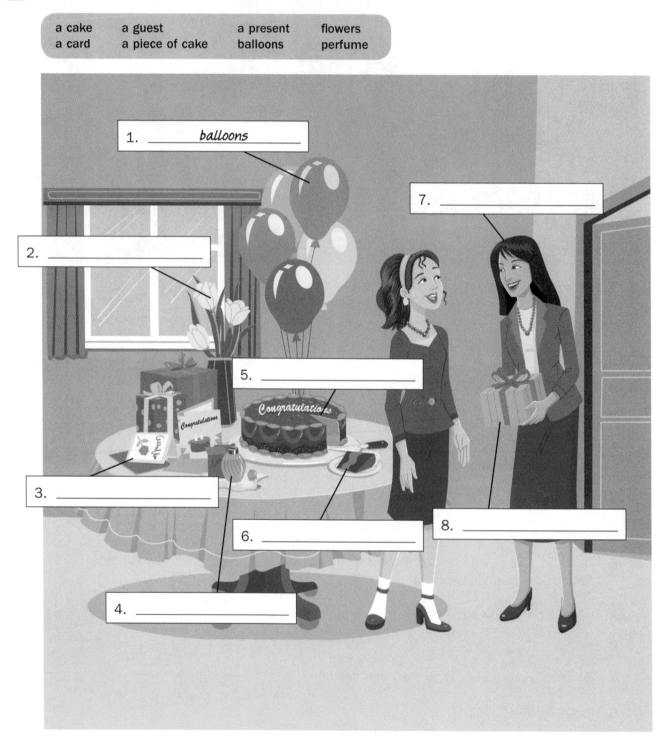

1. _____balloons_____

2. _____

3. _____

4. _____

5. _____

6. _____

7. _____

8. _____

## 2 Find the words.

| balloons | card | graduation | party | piece |
|----------|------|------------|-------|-------|
| cake | flowers | guest | perfume | present |

| g | p | a | r | t | y | p | p | p |
|---|---|---|---|---|---|---|---|---|
| r | r | e | t | a | e | g | s | i |
| a | e | p | a | y | u | u | b | e |
| d | s | i | c | g | p | e | a | c |
| u | e | c | a | k | e | s | l | e |
| a | n | b | r | s | r | t | l | p |
| t | t | n | d | a | f | i | o | a |
| i | e | r | f | s | u | n | o | f |
| o | u | c | y | l | m | t | n | t |
| n | f | l | o | w | e | r | s | a |

## 3 Listen. Circle T (True) or F (False).

**Conversation A**

1. Amy is having a graduation party.    (T)    F
2. Amy's dad made the cake.    T    F
3. Uncle Lee brought Amy some perfume.    T    F

**Conversation B**

4. Ms. Landers is Amy's teacher.    T    F
5. Uncle Lee is playing with his children.    T    F
6. Amy is going to get the children some water.    T    F

**Conversation C**

7. Sophie is Amy's sister.    T    F
8. Amy's sister is at the party.    T    F
9. Danny's card is funny.    T    F

# Lesson B  Would you like some cake?

Study the chart on page 130.

## 1  Read the answers. Write the questions.

1. **A** _Would you like some cake?_
                    some cake
   **B** Yes, I would.

2. **A** _____
                    some coffee
   **B** Yes, they would.

3. **A** _____
                    some ice cream
   **B** Yes, we would.

4. **A** _____
                    a balloon
   **B** Yes, she would.

5. **A** _____
                    some flowers
   **B** Yes, they would.

6. **A** _____
                    some dessert
   **B** Yes, I would.

7. **A** _____
                    a cup of tea
   **B** Yes, he would.

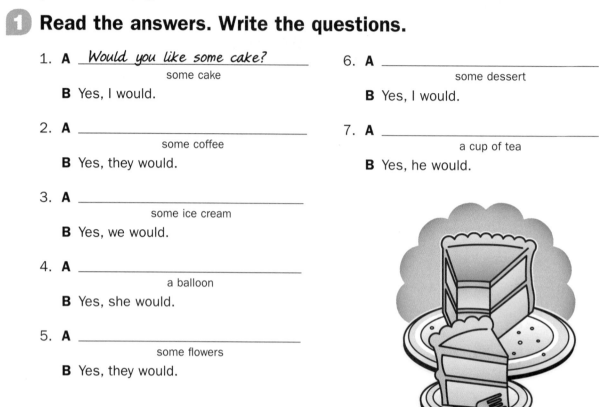

## 2  Read the questions. Circle the answers.

1. **A** Would you like some cake?
   **B** a. Yes, I would.
       b. I'd like some cake.

2. **A** What would you like?
   **B** a. Yes, please.
       b. I'd like some coffee, please.

3. **A** Would they like a cup of tea?
   **B** a. No, they wouldn't.
       b. No, I don't.

4. **A** What would she like?
   **B** a. She'd like it.
       b. She'd like a sandwich.

5. **A** Would they like some ice cream?
   **B** a. Yes, they would.
       b. They would like some soda.

6. **A** What would he like to drink?
   **B** a. He'd like some soda, please.
       b. Yes, he would.

7. **A** Would you like some coffee?
   **B** a. He'd like water, and I'd like tea.
       b. Yes, we would.

8. **A** What would you like to eat?
   **B** a. No, thank you.
       b. I'd like a piece of cake.

## 3 Look at the pictures. Complete the conversations.

1. **A** What would your friends like to drink?

   **B** _They'd like some soda._

2. **A** Would your husband like something to drink?

   **B** Yes, please. _____

3. **A** What would you and your husband like to eat?

   **B** _____

4. **A** Would your daughter like a sandwich?

   **B** No, thanks. But _____

5. **A** Would you like something to eat?

   **B** Yes, please. _____

6. **A** Would you like something to drink?

   **B** No, thanks. But _____

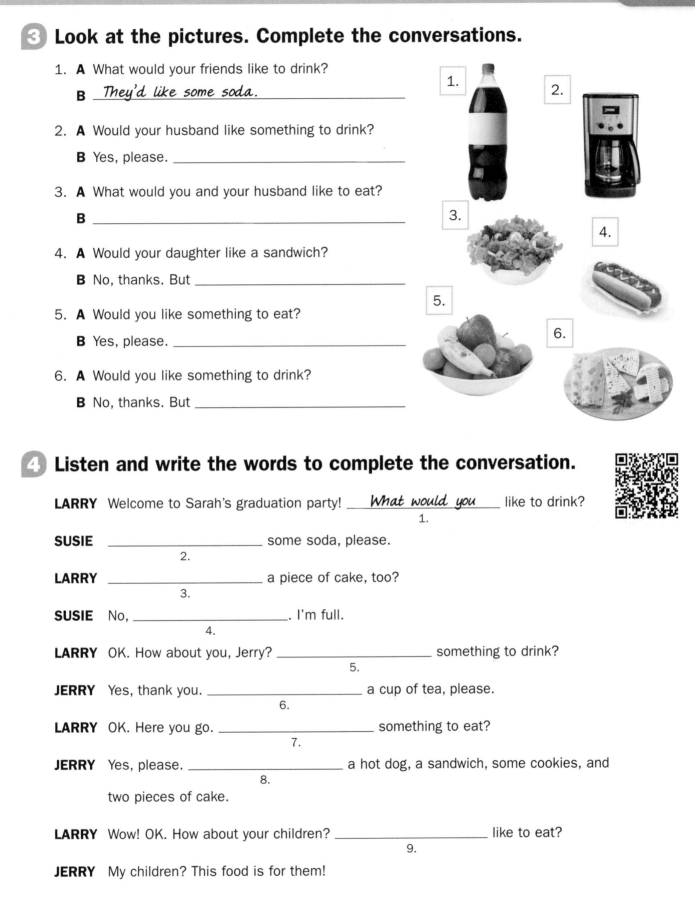

## 4 Listen and write the words to complete the conversation.

**LARRY** Welcome to Sarah's graduation party! _What would you_ like to drink?
1.

**SUSIE** _____ some soda, please.
2.

**LARRY** _____ a piece of cake, too?
3.

**SUSIE** No, _____. I'm full.
4.

**LARRY** OK. How about you, Jerry? _____ something to drink?
5.

**JERRY** Yes, thank you. _____ a cup of tea, please.
6.

**LARRY** OK. Here you go. _____ something to eat?
7.

**JERRY** Yes, please. _____ a hot dog, a sandwich, some cookies, and
8.

two pieces of cake.

**LARRY** Wow! OK. How about your children? _____ like to eat?
9.

**JERRY** My children? This food is for them!

# Lesson C Tim gave Mary a present.

Study the chart on page 130.

 **1 Rewrite the sentences.**

1. Tim gave a present to Mary.

   *Tim gave Mary a present.*

2. Jim bought some flowers for Sarah.

   _____

3. Elias wrote an email to his father.

   _____

4. Marta bought some soda for her son.

   _____

5. Felix gave some ice cream to his children.

   _____

6. Liu-na sent a birthday card to her mother.

   _____


**2 Answer the questions. Use *her*, *him*, or *them*.**

1. **A** What did Tim give Mary?

   **B** *Tim gave her a present.* _____

2. **A** What did Jim buy Sarah?

   **B** _____

3. **A** What did Elias write his father?

   **B** _____

4. **A** What did Marta buy her son?

   **B** _____

5. **A** What did Felix give his children?

   **B** _____

6. **A** What did Liu-na send her mother?

   **B** _____

**3** **Read the list of Mick and Mina's wedding presents. Complete the conversation.**

| Gift | From | Thank-you note |
|---|---|---|
| a check | Mina's parents | ✓ |
| a barbecue grill | Mick's brother | |
| a salad bowl | Maria | ✓ |
| coffee cups | Penny | |
| linens | Rod | |
| towels | Mina's sister | ✓ |

**MICK** Would you like some help?

**MINA** Yes, please. Could you write a thank-you note to your brother?

**MICK** OK. What did he give us?

**MINA** He gave us a ____barbecue grill____ .
1.

**MICK** Oh, that's right. OK. What about Maria? What did she give us?

**MINA** She gave us _____. But don't write her a thank-you note
2.
because I already wrote one. Could you write Rod a note?

**MICK** Sure. Did he give us the _____?
3.

**MINA** Yes. Did Penny give us the _____?
4.

**MICK** Yeah. They're nice! And look, your parents gave us _____.
5.

**4** **Answer the questions. Use *them*.**

1. Who gave Mick and Mina a check?
   _Mina's parents gave them a check._

2. Who gave Mick and Mina coffee cups?
   _____

3. What did Maria give Mick and Mina?
   _____

4. What did Mina's sister give Mick and Mina?
   _____

# Lesson D  Reading

**1  Read and answer the questions about the email. Then listen.**

| | |
|---|---|
| From: | Do-cheon Yoon <dyoon13@cup.org> |
| To: | Chi-ho Yoon <chyoon42@cup.org> |
| Date: | November 1, 2018 |
| Subject: | Halloween |

Hi Dad,

How are you? We're all great here. Last night was Halloween. Halloween is the children's favorite holiday. It was a lot of fun. The children made their own costumes. I took the children "trick-or-treating," and Yuni stayed home to give out candy. Over a hundred children came to our house for candy! After we got home, our children ate some candy, and then they went to bed. It will probably take about a month to eat all the candy!

Love,

Do-cheon

1. What is the children's favorite holiday? *Halloween* _____

2. When was Halloween? _____

3. Who made the children's costumes? _____

4. Who went "trick-or-treating" with the children? _____

5. What did Yuni do? _____

6. How long will it take to eat all the candy? _____

**2  Match the celebrations with the items.**

1. Thanksgiving __*d*__          a. white dress

2. a wedding _____             b. presents for mothers

3. Valentine's Day _____       c. presents for a house

4. New Year's Eve _____        d. turkey for dinner

5. Mother's Day _____          e. barbecues and fireworks

6. a baby shower _____         f. candy and costumes for children

7. a housewarming _____        g. parties until midnight

8. Halloween _____             h. presents for babies

9. Independence Day _____      i. chocolates, flowers, and cards with red hearts

## 3 Read the sentences. What was the celebration?

1. I wore a beautiful white dress. There were flowers everywhere.
People gave us beautiful presents. *a wedding*_____

2. We went to my grandmother's house. She cooked us a big
turkey dinner. _____

3. The children went to all the houses in the neighborhood. The neighbors
gave them candy. _____

4. Last Sunday, my children brought me breakfast in bed. _____

5. We went to a big party. At midnight we celebrated. We went home
at 1:00 a.m. _____

6. People gave us clothes and toys for our new baby. _____

## 4 Complete the chart. Use some celebrations more than once.

| a baby shower | a wedding | Mother's Day | Thanksgiving |
| a housewarming | Independence Day | New Year's Eve | Valentine's Day |

| Parties | No school or work | Give presents or cards |
|---|---|---|
| *a baby shower* | | *a baby shower* |
| | | |
| | | |
| | | |

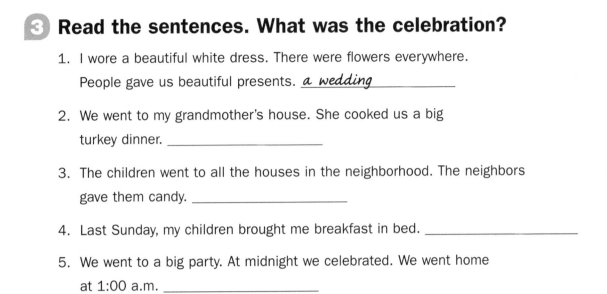

# Lesson E Writing

## 1 Write sentences.

1. the / for / interesting / you / Thank you / book / me / gave / .
   _Thank you for the interesting book you gave me._

2. reading / excited / really / I'm / it / about / .
   _____

3. Thank you / for / cake / to / party / bringing / a / our / .
   _____

4. really / I / liked / a lot / it / .
   _____

5. to / coming / for / Thank you / my / party / graduation / .
   _____

6. you / hope / I / good / had / time / a / .
   _____

## 2 Complete the thank-you note. Use the sentences from Exercise 1.

> June 15, 2018
>
> Dear Erica,
>
> _Thank you for the interesting book you gave me_ .
>                          1.
> _____ . It looks really good.
>                   2.
> Also, _____ .
>                        3.
> _____ . Chocolate is my favorite kind of cake!
>         4.
> _____ .
>                  5.
> _____ . I had a very
>              6.
> good time! I hope to see you soon.
>
>                          Sincerely,
>                          Joe

**3** **Answer the questions. Use the information from Exercises 1 and 2.**

1. Whose party was it?

   *It was Joe's party.*

2. When did Joe write the thank-you note?

   _____

3. Who did Joe write the thank-you note to?

   _____

4. What did Erica give Joe?

   _____

5. What did Erica bring to the party?

   _____

6. Why did Joe like the cake?

   _____

**4** **Read the story. Complete the thank-you note.**

chocolates   Dan   favorite   hope   Thank you   Valentine's Day

Dan visited Leanne on Valentine's Day. He gave Leanne a box of chocolates. They were Leanne's favorite kind of candy. She wrote him a note two days later.

February 16, 2018

Dear _____*Dan*_____,
            1.

   Thank you for the _____ you gave me for _____.
                          2.                              3.

They were delicious! They are my _____ kind.
                                    4.

_____ so much for visiting me on Valentine's Day.
     5.

I _____ you had fun.
     6.

                              Sincerely,
                              Leanne

**1  Read the questions. Look at the invitation. Fill in the correct answers.**

Inbox (New Message)

RSVP by April 12

**A Day in the Park**
**Barbecue**

**Host:** Sheila Cristal
**Where:** Tucker's Grove Park
**When:** Saturday, April 14, 11:00–4:00
Come and celebrate **Paco's 18th birthday.**
Bring something to barbecue for lunch.
Children and pets welcome!

**Guest List**
How many people, as of April 13?
• Yes 25   • No 5   • Maybe 0

to RSVP, CLICK HERE!

1. What is this?

   ● It's an email invitation.

   B It's an email thank-you card.

   C It's a paper invitation.

   D It's an RSVP to an invitation.

2. When is the party?

   A April 12

   B April 13

   C April 14

   D April 18

3. What kind of party is it?

   A a birthday party

   B a children's party

   C a graduation party

   D a lunch party

4. How long is the party?

   A four hours

   B five hours

   C six hours

   D seven hours

5. How many guests are coming?

   A 0

   B 5

   C 25

   D 30

6. Which statement is true?

   A Paco is giving the party.

   B Guests should not bring their dogs.

   C Guests should bring gifts.

   D Sheila is giving the party.

7. What should people bring to the party?

   A something to barbecue

   B something to drink

   C flowers and gifts

   D all of the above

8. When do people need to say yes or no?

   A by 4/12

   B by 4/14

   C by 4/15

   D by 12/4

**2** **Complete the sentences about the pictures. Use *there is, there isn't any, there are, there aren't any, there was, there wasn't any, there were,* and *there weren't any*.**

**Mom's graduation party – 1997**

1. _____*There were*_____ six people at the party.

2. _____ a small cake on the table.

3. _____ flowers on the table.

4. _____ fruit on the table.

5. _____ ice cream on the table.

6. _____ balloons on the table.

**My graduation party – Today**

7. _____*There are*_____ twelve people at the party.

8. _____ a large cake on the table.

9. _____ flowers on the table.

10. _____ fruit on the table.

11. _____ ice cream on the table.

12. _____ balloons on the table.

# REFERENCE

## Present continuous

Use the present continuous for actions happening now and in the near future.

### WH- QUESTIONS

| What | am | I | doing now? |
|------|-----|------|------------|
|      | are | you |            |
|      | is | he |             |
|      | is | she |            |
|      | is | it |             |
|      | are | we |            |
|      | are | you |            |
|      | are | they |           |

### ANSWERS

| You're | working. |
|--------|----------|
| I'm    |          |
| He's   |          |
| She's  |          |
| It's   |          |
| You're |          |
| We're  |          |
| They're |         |

**Contractions**

| I'm | = | I am |
|-----|---|------|
| You're | = | You are |
| He's | = | He is |
| She's | = | She is |
| It's | = | It is |
| We're | = | We are |
| You're | = | You are |
| They're | = | They are |

## Simple present

Use the simple present for repeated, usual, or daily actions.

### YES / NO QUESTIONS

| Do | I | work? |
|------|------|-------|
| Do | you |      |
| Does | he |     |
| Does | she |    |
| Does | it |     |
| Do | we |       |
| Do | you |      |
| Do | they |     |

### SHORT ANSWERS

| Yes, | you | do. |
|------|------|------|
|      | I | do. |
|      | he | does. |
|      | she | does. |
|      | it | does. |
|      | you | do. |
|      | we | do. |
|      | they | do. |

| No, | you | don't. |
|------|------|--------|
|      | I | don't. |
|      | he | doesn't. |
|      | she | doesn't. |
|      | it | doesn't. |
|      | you | don't. |
|      | we | don't. |
|      | they | don't. |

### WH- QUESTIONS: WHAT

| What | do | I | do every day? |
|------|------|------|----------------|
|      | do | you |               |
|      | does | he |               |
|      | does | she |              |
|      | does | it |               |
|      | do | we |                |
|      | do | you |               |
|      | do | they |              |

### ANSWERS

| You | usually | work. |
|------|---------|-------|
| I |         | work. |
| He |        | works. |
| She |       | works. |
| It |        | works. |
| You |       | work. |
| We |        | work. |
| They |      | work. |

### WH- QUESTIONS: WHEN

| When | do | I | usually work? |
|------|------|------|----------------|
|      | do | you |               |
|      | does | he |               |
|      | does | she |              |
|      | do | we |                |
|      | do | you |               |
|      | do | they |              |

### ANSWERS

| You | usually | work | on Friday. |
|------|---------|------|------------|
| I |         | work |            |
| He |        | works |           |
| She |       | works |           |
| You |       | work |            |
| We |        | work |            |
| They |      | work |            |

## Simple present of *want* and *need*

**WH- QUESTIONS: WHAT**

| What | do | I | want | to do? |
|------|------|------|------|------|
| | do | you | | |
| | does | he | | |
| | does | she | | |
| | do | we | | |
| | do | you | | |
| | do | they | | |

| What | do | I | need | to do? |
|------|------|------|------|------|
| | do | you | | |
| | does | he | | |
| | does | she | | |
| | do | we | | |
| | do | you | | |
| | do | they | | |

**ANSWERS**

| You | want | to go home. |
|------|------|------|
| I | want | |
| He | wants | |
| She | wants | |
| You | want | |
| We | want | |
| They | want | |

| You | need | to go home. |
|------|------|------|
| I | need | |
| He | needs | |
| She | needs | |
| You | need | |
| We | need | |
| They | need | |

## Simple present of *have to* + verb

**WH- QUESTIONS: WHAT**

| What | do | I | have to | do? |
|------|------|------|------|------|
| | do | you | | |
| | does | he | | |
| | does | she | | |
| | does | it | | |
| | do | we | | |
| | do | you | | |
| | do | they | | |

**ANSWERS**

| You | have to | go home. |
|------|------|------|
| I | have to | |
| He | has to | |
| She | has to | |
| It | has to | |
| You | have to | |
| We | have to | |
| They | have to | |

## Simple present with *Which* questions

**WH- QUESTIONS: WHICH**

| Which plumber | do | I | recommend? |
|------|------|------|------|
| | do | you | |
| | does | he | |
| | does | she | |
| | does | it | |
| | do | we | |
| | do | you | |
| | do | they | |

**ANSWERS**

| You | recommend | Joe's Plumbing. |
|------|------|------|
| I | recommend | |
| He | recommends | |
| She | recommends | |
| It | recommends | |
| You | recommend | |
| We | recommend | |
| They | recommend | |

*Qual encanador você recomende ?*

## Simple past with regular and irregular verbs

Use the simple past for actions completed in the past.

*WH- QUESTIONS: WHAT*

| What | did | I / you / he / she / it / we / you / they | do? |
|------|-----|-------------------------------------------|-----|

| AFFIRMATIVE STATEMENTS | | NEGATIVE STATEMENTS | | |
|---|---|---|---|---|
| I / You / He / She / It / We / You / They | stayed. / ate. | I / You / He / She / It / We / You / They | didn't | stay. / eat. |

didn't = did not

| YES / NO QUESTIONS | | | SHORT ANSWERS | | | | | |
|---|---|---|---|---|---|---|---|---|
| Did | I / you / he / she / it / we / you / they | stay? / eat? | Yes, | you / I / he / she / it / you / we / they | did. | No, | you / I / he / she / it / you / we / they | didn't. |

| WH- QUESTIONS: *WHEN* | | | | ANSWERS | | |
|---|---|---|---|---|---|---|
| When | did | I / you / he / she / it / we / you / they | move? / leave? | You / I / He / She / It / You / We / They | moved / left | last week. |

| WH- QUESTIONS: *WHERE* | | | | ANSWERS | | |
|---|---|---|---|---|---|---|
| Where | did | I / you / he / she / it / we / you / they | go? | You / I / He / She / It / You / We / They | stayed / went | home. |

## Future with *will*

Use *will* for a prediction or promise in the future.

*WH- QUESTIONS: WHAT*

| What | will | I you he she we you they | do | tomorrow? |
|------|------|--------------------------|----|-----------|

**AFFIRMATIVE STATEMENTS**

| I'll You'll He'll She'll We'll You'll They'll | probably | work. |
|-----------------------------------------------|----------|-------|

'll = will

**NEGATIVE STATEMENTS**

| I You He She We You They | won't | work. |
|--------------------------|-------|-------|

won't = will not

## Future with *be going to*

Use *be going to* for a plan or prediction in the future.

*WH- QUESTIONS*

| What | am are is is are are | I you he she we you they | going to do tomorrow? |
|------|----------------------|--------------------------|-----------------------|

**AFFIRMATIVE STATEMENTS**

| I'm You're He's She's We're You're They're | going to | play soccer. |
|--------------------------------------------|----------|--------------|

**NEGATIVE STATEMENTS**

| I'm You're He's She's We're You're They're | not going to | play soccer. |
|--------------------------------------------|--------------|--------------|

## *Should*

*WH- QUESTIONS: WHAT*

| What | should | I you he she we you they | do? |
|------|--------|--------------------------|-----|

**AFFIRMATIVE STATEMENTS**

| I You He She We You They | should | take medicine. |
|--------------------------|--------|----------------|

**NEGATIVE STATEMENTS**

| I You He She We You They | shouldn't | take medicine. |
|--------------------------|-----------|----------------|

shouldn't = should not

## Would you like . . . ?

### YES / NO QUESTIONS

| | | | |
|---|---|---|---|
| | you | | |
| | he | | |
| Would | she | like | some cake? |
| | you | | |
| | they | | |

### SHORT ANSWERS

| | | |
|---|---|---|
| | I | |
| | he | |
| Yes, | she | would. |
| | we | |
| | they | |

### WH- QUESTIONS: WHAT

| | | | |
|---|---|---|---|
| | | you | |
| | | he | |
| What | would | she | like? |
| | | you | |
| | | they | |

### ANSWERS

| | | |
|---|---|---|
| I'd | | |
| He'd | | |
| She'd | like | some cake. |
| We'd | | |
| They'd | | |

'd = would

## Direct and indirect objects

| | |
|---|---|
| | me. |
| | you. |
| | him. |
| | her. |
| Tim gave a present to | Mary. |
| | it. |
| | us. |
| | you. |
| | them. |

| | | |
|---|---|---|
| | me | |
| | you | |
| | him | |
| | her | |
| Tim gave | Mary | a present. |
| | it | |
| | us | |
| | you | |
| | them | |

## Simple past irregular verbs

| | | | | | | | | |
|---|---|---|---|---|---|---|---|---|
| be | → | was / were | eat | → | ate | know | → | knew |
| become | → | became | fall | → | fell | leave | → | left |
| begin | → | began | feel | → | felt | lose | → | lost |
| break | → | broke | fight | → | fought | make | → | made |
| bring | → | brought | find | → | found | meet | → | met |
| build | → | built | fly | → | flew | pay | → | paid |
| buy | → | bought | forget | → | forgot | put | → | put |
| catch | → | caught | give | → | gave | read | → | read |
| choose | → | chose | go | → | went | ride | → | rode |
| come | → | came | have | → | had | run | → | ran |
| cost | → | cost | hear | → | heard | say | → | said |
| cut | → | cut | hide | → | hid | see | → | saw |
| do | → | did | hold | → | held | sell | → | sold |
| drink | → | drank | hurt | → | hurt | send | → | sent |
| drive | → | drove | keep | → | kept | sing | → | sang |

| | | |
|---|---|---|
| sit | → | sat |
| sleep | → | slept |
| speak | → | spoke |
| spend | → | spent |
| stand | → | stood |
| steal | → | stole |
| swim | → | swam |
| take | → | took |
| teach | → | taught |
| tell | → | told |
| think | → | thought |
| understand | → | understood |
| wake | → | woke |
| wear | → | wore |
| write | → | wrote |

# Comparative and superlative adjectives

| | Adjective | Comparative | Superlative |
|---|---|---|---|
| Adjectives with one syllable | cheap<br>large<br>long<br>new<br>nice<br>old<br>short<br>small<br>tall<br>young | cheaper<br>larger<br>longer<br>newer<br>nicer<br>older<br>shorter<br>smaller<br>taller<br>younger | the cheapest<br>the largest<br>the longest<br>the newest<br>the nicest<br>the oldest<br>the shortest<br>the smallest<br>the tallest<br>the youngest |
| Adjectives with one syllable ending in a vowel-consonant pair | big<br>fat<br>hot<br>sad | bigger<br>fatter<br>hotter<br>sadder | the biggest<br>the fattest<br>the hottest<br>the saddest |
| Adjectives with two or more syllables | beautiful<br>comfortable<br>crowded<br>expensive | more beautiful<br>more comfortable<br>more crowded<br>more expensive | the most beautiful<br>the most comfortable<br>the most crowded<br>the most expensive |
| Adjectives ending in -y | friendly<br>heavy<br>pretty | friendlier<br>heavier<br>prettier | the friendliest<br>the heaviest<br>the prettiest |
| Irregular adjectives | good<br>bad | better<br>worse | the best<br>the worst |

# Adjective word order

| Size | Age | Shape | Color | Pattern |
|---|---|---|---|---|
| big<br>large<br>long<br>medium<br>short<br>small | modern<br>new<br>old | curly<br>oval<br>round<br>square<br>straight | black<br>blue<br>brown<br>green<br>purple<br>red<br>white<br>yellow | checked<br>plaid<br>polka dotted<br>striped |

## Examples

*He's wearing a modern purple and yellow striped tie.*
*She has a large square brown coffee table.*
*They have a medium-sized old green car.*

# ANSWER KEY

## Welcome

### Exercise 1A  page 2
1. is reading
2. is using
3. is talking
4. are writing
5. is helping

### Exercise 1B  page 2
1. No, she isn't
2. Yes, he is
3. No, she isn't
4. No, they aren't
5. Yes, she is
6. Yes, he is

### Exercise 2A  page 3
1. False; Ivan can't cook.
2. True
3. False; Ivan and Irma can't speak Chinese.
4. True
5. False; Joe can't swim.
6. True
7. False; Oscar and Lara can't use a computer.
8. False; Irma can drive a truck.

### Exercise 2B  page 3
speak English, speak Chinese, write Chinese, cook

### Exercise 3A  page 4
1. is
2. am
3. is
4. is
5. are
6. is
7. is
8. were
9. weren't
10. were
11. are
12. are
13. was
14. am
15. was
16. is
17. are
18. are

### Exercise 3B  page 4
1. My name is Diego. I am from Mexico. I was a truck driver in Mexico. I am married. There are five people in my family.
2. My name is Bae. I am from Korea. I was a student in Korea. I am not married. There are two people in my family.

### Exercise 4A  page 5
1. work
2. went
3. goes
4. came
5. had
6. went
7. worked
8. didn't go
9. take
10. slept
11. didn't take
12. walked
13. visit
14. go
15. went
16. celebrated

### Exercise 4B  page 5
1. slept
2. works
3. takes
4. visited
5. walked
6. went
7. celebrates
8. didn't buy

## Unit 1: Personal information

### Lesson A: Listening

### Exercise 1  page 6
1. curly hair
2. short brown hair
3. a jogging suit
4. striped pants
5. short blond hair
6. long brown hair
7. a white T-shirt
8. a long skirt

### Exercise 2  page 6
1. curly hair
2. striped pants
3. short blond hair
4. a white T-shirt
5. short brown hair
6. a jogging suit
7. long brown hair
8. a long skirt

### Exercise 3  page 7
**Hair color**
black
blond
brown
**Hair length**
long
short
**Hair type**
curly
straight

### Exercise 4  page 7
1. b
2. a
3. a
4. c
5. a
6. c

### Lesson B: She's wearing a short plaid skirt.

### Exercise 1  page 8
1. a green and white striped dress
2. a black and blue checked shirt
3. a long blue coat
4. small red and yellow shoes
5. black plaid pants
6. short brown boots

### Exercise 2  page 8
1. a long blue coat
2. small white and black shoes
3. short brown boots
4. black plaid pants
5. a black and blue checked shirt
6. a green and white striped dress

### Exercise 3  page 9
1. a
2. c
3. b
4. c
5. a
6. b

### Exercise 4  page 9
| Colors | Sizes |
|---|---|
| black | large |
| green | long |
| purple | short |
| red | small |

**Clothing**
coat
jeans
pants
sweater

### Lesson C: What are you doing right now?

### Exercise 1  page 10
1. b
2. a
3. b
4. a
5. a
6. b

### Exercise 2  page 10
1A. do, do
1B. study
1A. are, doing
1B. am reading
2A. is, doing
2B. is playing
2A. does, do
2B. plays
3A. does, do
3B. works
3A. is, doing
3B. is watching

### Exercise 3  page 11
1. a
2. a
3. b
4. b
5. a
6. b

### Exercise 4  page 11
1. leaves
2. goes
3. calls
4. talk
5. sits
6. studies

### Exercise 5  page 11
1. is relaxing
2. is watching
3. are sitting
4. is drinking
5. is wearing
6. is speaking

### Lesson D: Reading

### Exercise 1  page 12
**Present continuous**
am writing
are working
am wearing

**Simple present**

| | |
|---|---|
| think | go |
| miss | wears |
| is | goes |

**Exercise 2** page 12
1. She's in the lunchroom.
2. She lives in Chicago.
3. She lives in New York.
4. He wears a uniform.
5. She wears jeans.
6. She's writing an email.

**Exercise 3** page 13

```
t f d b a w t o m d e a
e t g l o v e s d n a v
t n p c b e x u a p r p
i z z h a t a n c l r w
a n y r d o b g y m i a
n t d g m b e l p b n t
a p u r s e l a e h g c
x v r s k f t s s t s h
d v i n t i e s c a r f
h b n b r a c e l e t p
r a g i k j j s q w w c
t n e c k l a c e d d i
```

**Exercise 4** page 13

| | |
|---|---|
| 1. earrings | 7. purse |
| 2. scarf | 8. hat |
| 3. necklace | 9. sunglasses |
| 4. belt | 10. tie |
| 5. bracelet | 11. watch |
| 6. ring | 12. gloves |

**Lesson E: Writing**

**Exercise 1** page 14

**A**

| | |
|---|---|
| 1. green | 5. jacket |
| 2. goes | 6. earrings |
| 3. visits | 7. Norma |
| 4. watches | |

**B**

| | |
|---|---|
| 1. brown | 4. goes |
| 2. white | 5. plays |
| 3. jeans | 6. Sarah |

**C**

| | |
|---|---|
| 1. wearing | 5. goes |
| 2. shoes | 6. studies |
| 3. blond | 7. Martina |
| 4. blue | |

**Exercise 2** page 15
1. Bobby goes to New York City on the weekend.
2. Georgia is wearing a black scarf and a red coat.
3. Susana goes to work after school every Monday.
4. Mei's hair is long.
5. Martin is carrying his books in a backpack.
6. Christina is wearing a watch.

**Exercise 3** page 15
1. On the weekend, Mary teaches English.
2. Sam leaves early every night.
3. Alberto watches TV on Thursday.
4. On Saturday, Raquel plays soccer.
5. Every Sunday, Michael wears a suit.
6. Petra has a birthday party every June.

**Lesson F: Another view**

**Exercise 1** page 16

| | | |
|---|---|---|
| 1. C | 3. D | 5. C |
| 2. C | 4. A | 6. D |

**Exercise 2,** page 17
1. and Dan does, too
2. and Rob doesn't, either
3. but Rachel doesn't
4. and Rob does, too
5. and Luke doesn't, either
6. but Alicia doesn't
7. and Luke does, too
8. and Alicia doesn't, either
9. but Dan doesn't
10. and Rachel doesn't, either

# Unit 2: At school

**Lesson A: Listening**

**Exercise 1** page 18

| | |
|---|---|
| 1. a computer lab | 5. a student |
| 2. a lab instructor | 6. a mouse |
| 3. a monitor | 7. a keyboard |
| 4. a hall | |

**Exercise 2** page 18

| | |
|---|---|
| 1. keyboarding | 4. work |
| 2. instructor | 5. skill |
| 3. computer | 6. register |

**Exercise 3** page 19
1. Diego's English instructor.
2. Diego's computer lab instructor.
3. 555-23-0967.
4. Room H102.
5. MW 6:00–7:50 p.m.
6. Computer lab.

**Exercise 4** page 19

| | | |
|---|---|---|
| 1. F | 4. F | 7. T |
| 2. T | 5. F | 8. T |
| 3. F | 6. T | 9. F |

**Lesson B: What do you want to do?**

**Exercise 1** page 20

| | | |
|---|---|---|
| 1. f | 3. d | 5. c |
| 2. e | 4. b | 6. a |

**Exercise 2** page 20
1. needs to take
2. wants to go
3. wants to get
4. want to talk
5. need to learn
6. need to register

**Exercise 3** page 21
1. He needs to take an auto mechanics class.
2. She needs to take a driver education class.
3. You need to take a citizenship class.
4. He needs to go to Room 131.
5. I need to go to Room 231.
6. They need to take a computer technology class.

**Lesson C: What will you do?**

**Exercise 1** page 22

| | |
|---|---|
| 1. will | 4. will |
| 2. will | 5. won't |
| 3. won't | 6. will |

**Exercise 2** page 22
1. He'll work on Thursday.
2. He'll take a driving lesson on Tuesday.
3. He'll work on Friday.
4. He'll meet Lisa for lunch on Saturday.
5. He'll call his mother on Sunday.
6. He'll take an English class on Monday and Wednesday.

**Exercise 3** page 23
1. buy a house
2. go to the U.S.
3. open a business
4. study English
5. get a GED
6. take a vocational course

**Exercise 4** page 23
1. What will she do in five years?
2. What will he do next year?
3. What will you do tomorrow?
4. What will they do this weekend?

**Lesson D: Reading**

**Exercise 1** page 24
1. 18 months.
2. On March 14.
3. At City College.
4. Registration, the classes, and the certificate.
5. Teachers and current students.

**Exercise 2** page 24

| | | | |
|---|---|---|---|
| 1. b | 2. c | 3. c | 4. a |

**Exercise 3** page 25

1. e     3. a     5. c
2. d     4. b

**Exercise 4** page 25

1. computer networking
2. dental assisting
3. fitness training
4. criminal justice
5. veterinary assisting
6. nail care
7. home health care
8. counseling

## Lesson E: Writing

**Exercise 1** page 26

1. b     3. f     5. c
2. d     4. a     6. e

**Exercise 2** page 26

1. get a second job on the weekend
2. he has a new baby
3. talk to people about job possibilities
4. read the classified section of the newspaper
5. look for jobs online
6. two months

**Exercise 3** page 27

1. goal          4. Second
2. children      5. Third
3. First         6. year

**Exercise 4** page 27

1. She wants to help her children with their homework.
2. She needs to find an adult school.
3. She needs to practice her English every day.
4. She needs to volunteer with the Parent-Teacher Association (PTA) at her children's school.
5. She will be ready next year.

## Lesson F: Another view

**Exercise 1** page 28

1. B     3. A     5. D
2. D     4. C     6. B

**Exercise 2** page 29

1. I'm going to study at the library.
2. I'm having chicken.
3. I'm going to watch TV.
4. I'll get up at 6:00 a.m.
5. I'm registering for a class.
6. I'll take Criminal Justice 2.
7. I'm visiting friends.
8. I'll swim and hike.
9. I'm going to get a job.
10. I'm taking flowers.

# Unit 3: Friends and family

## Lesson A: Listening

**Exercise 1** page 30

1. smoke
2. groceries
3. broken-down car
4. overheated engine
5. worried man
6. trunk
7. hood

**Exercise 2** page 30

1. overheated engine
2. smoke
3. worried man
4. hood
5. groceries
6. trunk
7. broken-down car

**Exercise 3** page 31

1. worried      5. smoke
2. broke        6. engine
3. groceries    7. hood
4. trunk

## Lesson B: What did you do last weekend?

**Exercise 1** page 32

1. b     3. b     5. a
2. a     4. b     6. a

**Exercise 2** page 32

1. grilled       7. had
2. bought        8. watched
3. drove         9. met
4. ate          10. played
5. fixed        11. read
6. went         12. stayed

**Exercise 3** page 33

1. went          4. had
2. met           5. ate
3. played        6. drove

**Exercise 4** page 33

a. 5     c. 3     e. 1
b. 2     d. 4     f. 6

## Lesson C: When do you usually play soccer?

**Exercise 1** page 34

1. went          4. eats
2. watch         5. leave
3. cleaned       6. met

**Exercise 2** page 34

1. d     3. e     5. f     7. a
2. g     4. b     6. c     8. h

**Exercise 3** page 35

1. has           5. met
2. plays         6. gets
3. worked        7. eat
4. has           8. ate

**Exercise 4** page 35

1. They usually buy groceries on Thursday.
2. She took her English exam on Friday.
3. He usually meets his friends after work.
4. She went to a movie with her uncle on Monday.
5. He met his friends at 5:30.
6. He studied for an English test.

## Lesson D: Reading

**Exercise 1** page 36

1. d     3. b     5. a     7. a
2. c     4. d     6. d     8. a

**Exercise 2** page 37

1. the laundry   5. a bath
2. the dishes    6. a nap
3. lunch         7. dressed
4. the bed       8. up

**Exercise 3** page 37

1. make          5. did
2. got           6. did
3. do            7. do
4. do            8. takes

## Lesson E: Writing

**Exercise 1** page 38

1. Ana usually gets up first.
2. Ron got up first this morning.
3. Ana usually takes a bath every morning.
4. Ana didn't take a bath this morning.
5. Ed usually leaves for work at 7:20.
6. The children usually leave for school at 7:30.

**Exercise 2** page 39

1. She gets up at 6:00.
2. She gets dressed at 6:15.
3. She eats her breakfast at 7:10.
4. She does the dishes at 7:45.
5. She makes the children's beds at 7:15.
6. She leaves the house at 7:55.

**Exercise 3** page 39

1. Next, First, Finally
2. Finally, First, Next

### Exercise 4 page 39

1. Last Monday, I had a very bad morning. First, I woke up late. Next, I didn't have time for breakfast. Finally, I was late for work.
2. Last Sunday, my family went to the beach. First, we had a picnic lunch. Next, we relaxed all afternoon. Finally, we drove home for dinner.

### Lesson F: Another view

**Exercise 1 page 40**

1. C  3. A  5. D
2. D  4. C  6. B

**Exercise 2 page 41**

1. makes cookies
2. plays cards
3. cooks dinner
4. do housework
5. go dancing
6. make breakfast
7. plays soccer
8. goes shopping
9. does homework
10. plays basketball
11. does chores
12. plays computer games

## Unit 4: Health

### Lesson A: Listening

**Exercise 1 page 42**

1. injured hand   5. inhaler
2. crutches       6. X-ray
3. sprained ankle 7. painful knee
4. broken bone

**Exercise 2 page 42**

1. X-ray          5. crutches
2. broken bone    6. painful knee
3. injured hand   7. sprained ankle
4. inhaler

**Exercise 3 page 43**

1. sprained   4. X-ray
2. crutches   5. broken
3. injured    6. inhaler

**Exercise 4 page 43**

1. b  3. a  5. a
2. b  4. c  6. c

### Lesson B: You should go to the hospital.

**Exercise 1 page 44**

1. should     4. should
2. shouldn't  5. should
3. shouldn't  6. shouldn't

### Exercise 2 page 44

1. shouldn't, should
2. shouldn't, should
3. should, shouldn't
4. shouldn't, should
5. should, shouldn't
6. should, shouldn't

### Exercise 3 page 45

1. clothes  4. towel
2. break    5. sun
3. water    6. shade

### Exercise 4 page 45

1. should     4. should
2. shouldn't  5. should
3. should     6. shouldn't

### Lesson C: You have to see a doctor.

**Exercise 1 page 46**

1. has to   4. have to
2. has to   5. has to
3. have to  6. have to

**Exercise 2 page 46**

1. He has to use crutches.
2. She has to see the doctor.
3. He has to get an X-ray.
4. He has to fill out an accident report.
5. She has to take medicine.

**Exercise 3 page 47**

1. c  3. d  5. b
2. f  4. e  6. a

**Exercise 4 page 47**

1. prescription  5. refrigerator
2. do            6. morning
3. have to       7. food
4. medicine

### Lesson D: Reading

**Exercise 1 page 48**

1. a  3. c  5. a
2. b  4. b  6. d

**Exercise 2 page 49**

1. d  3. b  5. c
2. e  4. a

**Exercise 3 page 49**

1. She has a rash.
2. They have allergies.
3. He has a swollen knee.
4. He has chest pains.
5. She has chills.
6. He has a sprained wrist.

**Exercise 4 page 49**

1. hurt      4. cut
2. accident  5. medicine
3. chest

### Lesson E: Writing

**Exercise 1 page 50**

1. There were four accidents in August.
2. The waiter had a sprained ankle.
3. The cook burned his hand on August 10.
4. Mr. Engels cut his hand.
5. Ms. Perry had a sprained wrist.
6. The name of the restaurant is Sleepy Burgers.

**Exercise 2 page 50**

1. 3, 1, 2
2. 2, 1, 3

**Exercise 3 page 51**

1. burned    5. medicine
2. injuries  6. days
3. accident  7. shouldn't
4. has to    8. work

**Exercise 4 page 51**

1. Carlos Garcia was hurt.
2. He had burned hands.
3. He was hurt this afternoon / on May 9, 2013.
4. Yes, it was.
5. He can return to work on May 16, 2013.
6. The name of the restaurant is Fast Frank's Restaurant.

### Lesson F: Another view

**Exercise 1 page 52**

1. C  3. D  5. A
2. C  4. C  6. A

**Exercise 2 page 52**

1. tablets  3. product
2. doctor   4. drowsiness

**Exercise 3 page 53**

1. d, a, b
2. c, e
3. f

1. have to / must  4. have to / must
2. have to / must  5. must not
3. must not        6. don't have to

## Unit 5: Around town

### Lesson A: Listening

**Exercise 1 page 54**

1. a suitcase
2. an information desk
3. a waiting area
4. a track
5. a ticket booth
6. departures
7. arrivals

## Exercise 2 page 54
1. a ticket booth
2. a suitcase
3. an information desk
4. a track
5. a waiting area
6. departures
7. arrivals

## Exercise 3 page 55
1. b  3. f  5. a
2. d  4. c  6. e

## Exercise 4 page 55
1. F  4. F  7. F
2. T  5. T  8. T
3. T  6. F  9. T

## Lesson B: How often? How long?

### Exercise 1 page 56
1. a  2. a  3. b  4. c

### Exercise 2 page 57
1. f  3. b  5. d
2. a  4. e  6. c

### Exercise 3 page 57
1. How often do you drive to the beach?
   How long does it take?
2. How often do you walk to the park?
   How long does it take?
3. How often do you go downtown by bus?
   How long does it take?

## Lesson C: She often walks to school.

### Exercise 1 page 58
1. never     4. often
2. rarely    5. always
3. sometimes

### Exercise 2 page 58
1. often      7. sometimes
2. rarely     8. sometimes
3. always     9. rarely
4. never     10. often
5. always    11. often
6. never     12. rarely

### Exercise 3 page 59
1. He always walks to school.
2. He never drives to school.
3. He rarely eats lunch at 1:00 p.m.
4. He usually eats dinner at home.
5. He usually goes to sleep at 10:00 p.m.

### Exercise 4 page 59
1a. Yes    3a. No
1b. No     3b. Yes
2a. No
2b. Yes

## Lesson D: Reading

### Exercise 1 page 60
1. c  2. c  3. d  4. b

### Exercise 2 page 60
1. Mariam    3. know
2. at a hotel    4. Mariam

### Exercise 3 page 61
1. goes    6. buy
2. stays   7. take
3. takes   8. write
4. go      9. stays
5. go

### Exercise 4 page 61
6, 3, 2, 8, 5, 1, 7, 4
A  How often do you go on vacation?
B  I go on vacation once a year.
A  Where do you usually go?
B  I usually go to Denver to see my parents.
A  How long does it take to get there?
B  It usually takes about three hours by plane.
A  Do you always go by plane?
B  Oh, yes! It takes two days by car.

## Lesson E: Writing

### Exercise 1 page 62
1. How often do trains go to Miami?
2. How long does it take to get to San Francisco?
3. How long does it take to drive to Detroit?
4. How often does the bus go to Boston?
5. How often do you visit your relatives in Houston?
6. Where do you usually stay?

### Exercise 2 page 62
a. 5    c. 4    e. 2
b. 1    d. 6    f. 3

### Exercise 3 page 62
1. one hour and five minutes
2. one hour and forty-five minutes
3. nine minutes
4. one hour and seven minutes
5. half an hour (or 30 minutes)
6. one hour and twelve minutes

### Exercise 4 page 63
1. Every year    3. Rarely
2. One week      4. Very happy

### Exercise 5 page 63
1. goes        7. uses
2. takes       8. sleeps
3. leaves      9. takes
4. gets       10. talks
5. doesn't like 11. likes
6. are         12. doesn't like

## Lesson F: Another view

### Exercise 1 page 64
1. How often does the bus go?
   It goes every half hour.
2. How does Shen-hui get to school?
   Shen-hui gets to school by bicycle.
3. How long does it take to get from Shen-hui's house to school by bicycle?
   It takes 20 minutes.
4. How often does Phillipe arrive on time?
   Phillipe always arrives on time.
5. How long does it take to get from Sara's house to school by subway?
   It takes 22 minutes.
6. How does Zoe get to school?
   Zoe drives to school.

### Exercise 2 page 65
1. to        4. to
2. to the    5. to the
3. X

### Exercise 3 page 65
1. to the library    4. to work
2. upstairs          5. outside
3. to the bank       6. to the mall

# Unit 6: Time

## Lesson A: Listening

### Exercise 1 page 66
1. class picture    4. baby
2. family           5. photo album
3. graduation       6. wedding

### Exercise 2 page 66
1. photo album      4. wedding
2. graduation       5. class picture
3. family           6. baby

### Exercise 3 page 67
1. a  3. b  5. b
2. c  4. c

### Exercise 4 page 67
1. T  4. F  7. T
2. F  5. F  8. T
3. T  6. T  9. F

## Lesson B: When did you move here?

### Exercise 1 page 68
1. moved     6. started
2. had       7. got
3. began     8. left
4. studied   9. met
5. found    10. graduated

## Exercise 2  page 68
**Regular verbs**
moved
studied
started
graduated
**Irregular verbs**
had
began
found
got
left
met

## Exercise 3  page 68
1. I moved here in 2000.
2. Ken started college in September.
3. We met in 1988.
4. We got married in 1990.
5. They began taking English classes last year.
6. Norma left for vacation on Saturday.

## Exercise 4  page 69
1. When did Elsa meet Pablo?
2. When did they get married?
3. They had Gabriel in 1996.
4. When did they have Clara?
5. They left Guatemala in 2004.
6. They moved from Chicago to Detroit in 2006.
7. When did Elsa start taking ESL classes?
8. She got her driver's license in 2010.
9. Elsa started a new job in 2011.
10. Gabriel graduated from college in 2018.

## Lesson C: He graduated two years ago.

## Exercise 1  page 70
**ago**
four days
a week
two years
a month
six months
**in**
the afternoon
December
1999
July
the morning
**on**
March 23rd
May 9th
Wednesday
April 11th, 1990
Saturday

**at**
6:15
night
noon
half past four

## Exercise 2  page 70
1. last
2. on
3. at
4. ago
5. in
6. this
7. before
8. on
9. before
10. ago

## Exercise 3  page 71
1. last
2. on
3. at
4. before
5. in
6. ago
7. after
8. last

## Exercise 4  page 71
1. He took his driving test four days ago.
2. He shopped for his sister's graduation present last week.
3. He played basketball on Friday, May 15th.
4. He had a doctor's appointment at 4:30.
5. He took his books back to the library two days ago.

## Lesson D: Reading

## Exercise 1  page 72
1. immigrated
2. worked
3. started
4. studied
5. began
6. met
7. fell
8. got
9. got
10. found
11. started
12. had
13. decided

## Exercise 2  page 72
1. She immigrated ten years ago.
2. She started English classes after she came to the U.S.
3. She studied English for three years.
4. They got married three years ago.
5. They found jobs after they got married.

## Exercise 3  page 73
a. 5    c. 4    e. 6
b. 3    d. 1    f. 2

## Exercise 4  page 73
1. immigrated
2. fell in love
3. got married
4. got engaged
5. got promoted
6. started a business
7. had a baby
8. retire

## Lesson E: Writing

## Exercise 1  page 74
1. on
2. had
3. started
4. in
5. took
6. worked
7. In
8. learned
9. After
10. found
11. last
12. opened

## Exercise 2  page 74
1. b    3. f    5. c
2. d    4. a    6. e

## Exercise 3  page 75
1. On January 5, 2009, she left China.
She left China on January 5, 2009.
2. In February 2009, she began English classes.
She began English classes in February 2009.
3. For two years, she took English classes.
She took English classes for two years.
4. In September 2010, she began vocational school.
She began vocational school in September 2010.
5. In 2012, she graduated from vocational school.
She graduated from vocational school in 2012.
6. In September 2012, she found a job as a chef.
She found a job as a chef in 2012.
7. Last week, she opened her own restaurant.
She opened her own restaurant last week.

## Lesson F: Another view

## Exercise 1  page 76
1. B    3. B    5. C
2. A    4. A    6. D

## Exercise 2  page 77
1. anyone; no one
2. anyone; everyone
3. anyone; no one
4. anyone; someone
5. anyone; someone
6. anyone; everyone

# Unit 7: Shopping

## Lesson A: Listening

## Exercise 1  page 78
1. stove
2. salesperson
3. sofa
4. piano
5. customer
6. appliances
7. furniture
8. price tag

## Exercise 2 page 78

1. sofa
2. furniture
3. customer
4. stove
5. salesperson
6. price tag
7. piano
8. appliances

## Exercise 3 page 79

1. furniture
2. salesperson
3. customer
4. appliances
5. sofa
6. price tag
7. piano
8. stove

## Lesson B: The brown sofa is bigger.

### Exercise 1 page 80

1. bigger
2. better
3. heavier
4. more comfortable

### Exercise 2 page 80

1. more comfortable
2. prettier
3. more expensive
4. cheaper
5. bigger
6. heavier

### Exercise 3 page 81

1. The dining room table is bigger.
2. The red chairs are smaller.
3. The refrigerator is more expensive.
4. The blue desk is older.
5. The green sofa is longer.
6. The black lamp is shorter.

## Lesson C: The yellow chair is the cheapest.

### Exercise 1 page 82

1. more expensive, the most expensive
2. cheaper, the cheapest
3. friendlier, the friendliest
4. better, the best
5. newer, the newest
6. heavier, the heaviest
7. lower, the lowest
8. more beautiful, the most beautiful
9. prettier, the prettiest
10. more crowded, the most crowded
11. more comfortable, the most comfortable
12. nicer, the nicest

### Exercise 2 page 82

1. the lowest
2. the most comfortable
3. the best
4. the most expensive
5. the nicest
6. the prettiest

7. the cheapest
8. the most crowded
9. the heaviest

### Exercise 3 page 83

1. a small lamp, a smaller lamp, the smallest lamp
2. an expensive desk, a more expensive desk, the most expensive desk
3. a good TV, a better TV, the best TV

### Exercise 4 page 83

1. The evening skirt is the most expensive.
2. The evening skirt is the longest.
3. The jeans skirt is the cheapest.
4. The tennis skirt is the shortest.

## Lesson D: Reading

### Exercise 1 page 84

1. newest
2. big
3. best
4. beautiful
5. nicest
6. most expensive
7. oldest
8. cheaper
9. cheapest
10. small

### Exercise 2 page 84

1. The name of the store is Antique Alley.
2. It opened on May 1st.
3. The most expensive thing was a large mirror.
4. It's so expensive because it's old.
5. The cheapest thing was a small lamp.
6. It's so cheap because it's small.

### Exercise 3 page 85

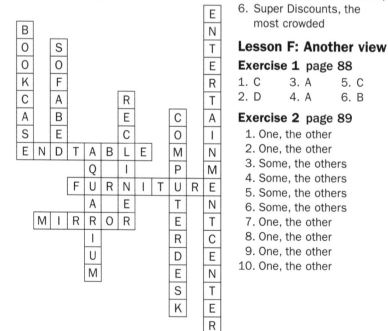

## Lesson E: Writing

### Exercise 1 page 86

1. The gift is for Miguel.
2. The gift is from his wife Amelia.
3. She gave him an airline ticket.
4. It's his 40th birthday.
5. He will go to Mexico City.
6. He will leave on August 10.

### Exercise 2 page 86

1. I bought the red sofa because it was the most comfortable.
2. Sandra gave her sister a pair of earrings because it was her birthday.
3. Mr. and Mrs. Chung shop at the Clothes Corner because it's the nicest store.
4. Roberto bought the brown recliner because it was on sale.
5. I bought an entertainment center because it was 50% off.

### Exercise 3 page 87

1. bigger
2. nicer
3. better
4. newer
5. more beautiful
6. higher
7. oldest
8. smallest
9. most crowded

### Exercise 4 page 87

1. Super Discounts, the smallest
2. Super Discounts, the oldest
3. Smart Department Store, the biggest
4. Smart Department Store, the most expensive
5. Best Discounts, the cheapest
6. Super Discounts, the most crowded

## Lesson F: Another view

### Exercise 1 page 88

1. C
2. D
3. A
4. A
5. C
6. B

### Exercise 2 page 89

1. One, the other
2. One, the other
3. Some, the others
4. Some, the others
5. Some, the others
6. Some, the others
7. One, the other
8. One, the other
9. One, the other
10. One, the other

# Unit 8: Work

## Lesson A: Listening

### Exercise 1 page 90
1. lab
2. orderly
3. co-workers
4. walker
5. linens
6. patient
7. supplies
8. wheelchair

### Exercise 2 page 90
1. lab
2. co-workers
3. linens
4. supplies
5. wheelchair
6. walker
7. orderly
8. patient

### Exercise 3 page 91
1. patient
2. co-workers
3. linens
4. wheelchair
5. orderly
6. walker

### Exercise 4 page 91
1. T
2. F
3. F
4. F
5. F
6. T
7. F
8. T
9. T

## Lesson B: Where did you go last night?

### Exercise 1 page 92
1. c
2. e
3. b
4. g
5. a
6. d
7. f

### Exercise 2 page 92
1. What
2. Where
3. What
4. What
5. Where
6. What
7. What
8. Where

### Exercise 3 page 93
1A. What
1B. They met new patients in the reception area.
2A. Where
2B. She took her patient to the lab.
3A. What
3B. He picked up X-rays from the lab.
4A. What
4B. made the bed in Room 304, delivered X-rays to the doctors.
5A. Where
5B. Jorge went to Room 310.
6A. What
6B. He helped a patient.
7A. What
7B. She took patients from the lab to their rooms.
8A. Where
8B. She went to the fourth floor.
9A. What
9B. He prepared rooms on the second floor.

## Lesson C: I work on Saturdays and Sundays.

### Exercise 1 page 94
1. and
2. or
3. but
4. and
5. but
6. or
7. and
8. and

### Exercise 2 page 94
1. Jun eats lunch at noon or at 1:00.
2. Javier helps the nurses and the doctors.
3. Tien picks up the supplies at the warehouse, but she doesn't deliver them.
4. Rieko met her new co-workers this morning, but she didn't meet any patients.
5. At the restaurant, Mustafa made the soup and the salad.
6. Anatoly drinks coffee or tea.

### Exercise 3 page 95
1. Dora went to the meeting, but she didn't take notes.
2. Adam checked the office email and went to the meeting.
3. Rachel prepared the meeting room, but she didn't make the coffee.
4. Dora and Adam went to the meeting, but they didn't prepare the meeting room.
5. Adam took notes and made copies.
6. Rachel picked up supplies and delivered the mail.

### Exercise 4 page 95
1. and
2. or
3. and
4. but

## Lesson D: Reading

### Exercise 1 page 96
1. c
2. b
3. c
4. a
5. b
6. a

### Exercise 2 page 96
1. Carrie McIntosh wrote the email.
2. She wrote it on May 25, 2018.
3. She teaches at Westport Community College.
4. She teaches in the Medical Assistant Certificate Program.
5. manage a medical office, schedule appointments, and take care of patient records

### Exercise 3 page 97
1. e
2. h
3. c
4. a
5. b
6. d
7. g
8. f

### Exercise 4 page 97
1. homemaker
2. construction worker
3. orderly
4. medical assistant
5. auto mechanic
6. teacher
7. cashier
8. cook

## Lesson E: Writing

### Exercise 1 page 98
1. works
2. makes
3. answers
4. takes
5. prepares
6. assists
7. worked
8. was
9. handled
10. operated
11. was
12. went
13. was
14. graduated
15. got

### Exercise 2 page 98
1. He started his job at the medical clinic in 2017.
2. He worked at Freshie's Pizza for 12 years.
3. He was a student from 2015 to 2017.
4. He studied for his GED at Staples Adult School.
5. He got his GED in June 2012.
6. He works at Valley Medical Clinic now.

### Exercise 3 page 99
1. I prepared food, but I didn't clear the tables.
2. I handled money and talked to people every day.
3. I helped the nurses, but I didn't help the doctors.
4. I took care of my children and my house.
5. I cleared tables and handled money, but I didn't prepare food.
6. I operated large machines and built houses.

### Exercise 4 page 99
a. 3: orderly
b. 1: cook
c. 5: busperson
d. 2: cashier
e. 6: construction worker
f. 4: homemaker

## Lesson F: Another view

### Exercise 1 page 100
1. Orderly
2. Cashier
3. Construction Worker
4. Medical Assistant
5. Auto Mechanic
6. Busperson

**Exercise 2** page 100

1. orderly
2. construction worker
3. cashier
4. auto mechanic
5. busperson
6. construction worker
7. medical assistant
8. busperson

**Exercise 3** page 101

1. couldn't, can
2. could, can't
3. couldn't, can't
4. could, can't
5. could, can
6. couldn't, can
7. couldn't, can
8. couldn't, can

# Unit 9: Daily living

## Lesson A: Listening

**Exercise 1** page 102

1. lightbulb
2. sink
3. dishwasher
4. leak
5. lock
6. garbage
7. washing machine
8. dryer

**Exercise 2** page 102

1. garbage
2. lock
3. lightbulb
4. sink
5. dishwasher
6. leak
7. washing machine
8. dryer

**Exercise 3** page 103

1. She has five appliances in her kitchen.
2. She has a washing machine, a dryer, a stove, a refrigerator, and a dishwasher.
3. Two appliances have problems.
4. The dishwasher and the washing machine have problems.

**Exercise 4** page 103

1. b
2. a
3. c
4. b
5. c
6. b
7. a
8. a
9. c

## Lesson B: Can you call a plumber, please?

**Exercise 1** page 104

1. Could you call a plumber, please?
2. Would you fix the window, please?
3. Will you fix the lock, please?
4. Would you fix the dryer, please?
5. Could you unclog the sink, please?
6. Can you fix the stove, please?

**Exercise 2** page 104

1. b
2. a
3. b
4. a
5. b
6. b

**Exercise 3** page 105

1. Could you fix the window, please?
2. Would you repair the refrigerator, please?
3. Can you fix the light, please?
4. Will you unclog the sink, please?
5. Could you repair the lock, please?
6. Would you fix the dishwasher, please?

**Exercise 4** page 105

1. Could you fix the light, please?
2. Could you unclog the bathtub, please?
3. Could you change the lightbulb, please?
4. Could you repair the dishwasher, please?
5. Could you clean the carpet, please?
6. Could you call a plumber, please?

## Lesson C: Which one do you recommend?

**Exercise 1** page 106

1. do; They recommend Jerry's Plumbing.
2. does; He recommends Joe Thompson.
3. do; I recommend Wired Electric.
4. do; They recommend Rite Price.
5. does; She recommends Bank and Trust.
6. does; He recommends SaveMore.

**Exercise 2** page 106

1. Marian recommends her cousin.
2. I suggest Drains R Us.
3. He likes Ed Peterson.
4. She recommends Dr. White.
5. We like Food City.
6. She recommends Rockland Adult School.
7. We suggest the City Clinic.

**Exercise 3** page 107

1. ABC
2. ABC
3. Fix It
4. Fix It

**Exercise 4** page 107

1. I recommend All Keys because it's open 24 hours.
2. They suggest Smitty's because it's licensed.
3. Harry likes All Keys because it's more experienced.
4. Muriel suggests Smitty's because it gives free keys.
5. They recommend All Keys because it has fast service.

## Lesson D: Reading

**Exercise 1** page 108

1. b
2. b
3. a
4. c
5. a
6. b

**Exercise 2** page 109

1. burned out
2. broken
3. dripping
4. bent
5. cracked
6. jammed
7. torn
8. scratched
9. stained

**Exercise 3** page 109

1. jammed
2. broken
3. burned out
4. dripping
5. torn
6. cracked
7. bent
8. stained
9. scratched

## Lesson E: Writing

**Exercise 1** page 110

1. broken
2. cracked
3. stained
4. jammed
5. burned out
6. dripping
7. scratched
8. clogged

**Exercise 2** page 110

1. Jim Bowen
2. 201, 412, 605, 822
3. Apartment Problems
4. Ms. Torrant
5. four
6. Jim Bowen

**Exercise 3** page 111

1. cracked bathtub
2. dishwasher
3. leaking
4. clogged toilet
5. stove
6. broken
7. carpet
8. stained

## Lesson F: Another view

**Exercise 1** page 112

1. C
2. A
3. D
4. B
5. C
6. D

**Exercise 2** page 113

1. Let's fix, let's fix
2. Let's buy, let's not buy, Let's clean
3. Let's buy, let's not buy, Let's make
4. Let's buy, Let's buy
5. Let's clean, Let's buy

# Unit 10: Free time

## Lesson A: Listening

**Exercise 1** page 114

1. balloons
2. flowers
3. a card
4. perfume
5. a cake
6. a piece of cake
7. a guest
8. a present

**Exercise 2** page 115

**Exercise 3** page 115

| | | |
|---|---|---|
| 1. T | 4. T | 7. F |
| 2. F | 5. F | 8. T |
| 3. F | 6. F | 9. T |

## Lesson B: Would you like some cake?

**Exercise 1** page 116

1. Would you like some cake?
2. Would they like some coffee?
3. Would you like some ice cream?
4. Would she like a balloon?
5. Would they like some flowers?
6. Would you like some dessert?
7. Would he like a cup of tea?

**Exercise 2** page 116

| | | | |
|---|---|---|---|
| 1. a | 3. a | 5. a | 7. b |
| 2. b | 4. b | 6. a | 8. b |

**Exercise 3** page 117

1. They'd like some soda.
2. He'd like some coffee.
3. We'd like some salad.
4. she'd like a hot dog.
5. I'd like some fruit.
6. I'd like some cheese.

**Exercise 4** page 117

1. What would you
2. I would like
3. Would you like
4. thank you
5. Would you like
6. I'd like
7. Would you like
8. I'd like
9. What would they

## Lesson C: Tim gave Mary a present.

**Exercise 1** page 118

1. Tim gave Mary a present.
2. Jim bought Sarah some flowers.
3. Elias wrote his father an email.
4. Marta bought her son some soda.

5. Felix gave his children some ice cream.
6. Liu-na sent her mother a birthday card.

**Exercise 2** page 118

1. Tim gave her a present.
2. Jim bought her some flowers.
3. Elias wrote him an email.
4. Marta bought him some soda.
5. Felix gave them some ice cream.
6. Liu-na sent her a birthday card.

**Exercise 3** page 119

1. barbecue grill     4. coffee cups
2. a salad bowl      5. a check
3. linens

**Exercise 4** page 119

1. Mina's parents gave them a check.
2. Penny gave them coffee cups.
3. Maria gave them a salad bowl.
4. Mina's sister gave them towels.

## Lesson D: Reading

**Exercise 1** page 120

1. Halloween
2. Last night
3. The children
4. Do-cheon
5. Stayed home and gave out candy
6. About a month

**Exercise 2** page 120

| | | |
|---|---|---|
| 1. d | 4. g | 7. c |
| 2. a | 5. b | 8. f |
| 3. i | 6. h | 9. e |

**Exercise 3** page 121

1. A wedding
2. Thanksgiving
3. Halloween
4. Mother's Day
5. New Year's Eve
6. A baby shower

**Exercise 4** page 121

**Parties**
a baby shower
a housewarming
New Year's Eve
a wedding
**No school or work**
Independence Day
Thanksgiving
**Give presents or cards**
a baby shower
a housewarming
Mother's Day
Valentine's Day
a wedding

## Lesson E: Writing

**Exercise 1** page 122

1. Thank you for the interesting book you gave me.
2. I'm really excited about reading it.
3. Thank you for bringing a cake to our party.
4. I really liked it a lot.
5. Thank you for coming to my graduation party.
6. I hope you had a good time.

**Exercise 2** page 122

1. Thank you for the interesting book you gave me.
2. I'm really excited about reading it.
3. thank you for bringing a cake to our party.
4. I really liked it a lot.
5. Thank you for coming to my graduation party.
6. I hope you had a good time.

**Exercise 3** page 123

1. It was Joe's party.
2. He wrote it on June 15, 2013.
3. He wrote it to Erica.
4. Erica gave him a book.
5. Erica brought a chocolate cake to the party.
6. Joe liked the cake because chocolate is his favorite kind of cake.

**Exercise 4** page 123

1. Dan
2. chocolates
3. Valentine's Day
4. favorite
5. Thank you
6. hope

## Lesson F: Another view

**Exercise 1** page 124

| | | | |
|---|---|---|---|
| 1. A | 3. A | 5. C | 7. A |
| 2. C | 4. B | 6. D | 8. A |

**Exercise 2** page 125

1. There were
2. There was
3. There were
4. There was
5. There wasn't any
6. There weren't any
7. There are
8. There is
9. There aren't any
10. There isn't any
11. There is
12. There are

# ACKNOWLEDGEMENTS

The authors and publishers acknowledge the following sources of copyright material and are grateful for the permissions granted. While every effort has been made, it has not always been possible to identify the sources of all the material used, or to trace all copyright holders. If any omissions are brought to our notice, we will be happy to include the appropriate acknowledgments on reprinting and in the next update to the digital edition, as applicable.

Key: T = Top, TL = Top Left, TC = Top Center, TR = Top Right, B = Below, BL = Below Left, BC = Below Center, BR = Below Right, C = Center, CL = Center Left, C = Center Right, T = Top, Ex = Exercise.

**Photo:**

All photos are sourced from Getty Images.

p. 4 (T): JGI/Jamie Grill/Blend Images; p. 4 (C): Klaus Tiedge/Blend Images; p. 4 (B): XiXinXing; p. 7: Squaredpixels/iStock/Getty Images Plus; p. 19: izusek/E+; p. 21 (Ex 3.1): DonNichols/E+; p. 21 (Ex 3.2): kropic/iStock/Getty Images Plus; p. 21 (Ex 3.3): Johner Images; p.21 (Ex 3.4): Fuse/Corbis; p. 24: Hero Images; p. 25 (Ex 4.1): bjdlzx/iStock/Getty Images Plus; p. 25 (Ex 4.2): bluecinema/E+; p. 25 (Ex 4.3): Michal Venera/Photolibrary; p. 25 (Ex 4.4): dcdebs/iStock/Getty Images Plus; p. 25 (Ex 4.5): Peter Muller/Cultura; p. 25 (Ex 4.6): Eric Audras/ONOKY; p. 25 (Ex 4.7): Blend Images - JGI/Tom Grill/ Brand X Pictures; p. 25 (Ex 4.8), p. 78 (Ex 2.2): KatarzynaBialasiewicz/iStock/Getty Images Plus; p. 26: Martin Barraud/OJO Images; p. 27: Ramiro Olaciregui/Moment; p. 29: Monashee Frantz/OJO Images; p. 39 (T): Rosa Images/Caiaimage; p. 39 (B): Ronnie Kaufman/Blend Images; p. 43: Wavebreakmedia/iStock/Getty Images Plus; p. 45: Olga Rozenbajgier/Canopy; p. 47: Antonio_Diaz/iStock/Getty Images Plus; p. 63 (T): richiesd/iStock/Getty Images Plus; p. 63 (B): Susanne Kronholm; p. 65 (Ex 3.1): monkeybusinessimages/iStock/Getty Images Plus; p. 65 (Ex 3.2): MangoStar_Studio/iStock/Getty Images Plus; p. 65 (Ex 3.3): Hola Images/Photolibrary; p. 65 (Ex 3.4): Andersen Ross/Blend Images; p. 65 (Ex 3.5): Richard Newstead/Moment; p. 65 (Ex 3.6): Gary Yeowell/The Image Bank; p. 67: Plush Studios/Bill Reitzel/Blend Images; p. 69: Jetta Productions/Blend Images; p. 77: Hill Street Studios/Blend Images; p. 78 (Ex 2.1): creativesunday2016/iStock/Getty Images Plus; p. 78 (Ex 2.3): Hero Images; p. 78 (Ex 2.4): ppart/iStock/Getty Images Plus; p. 78 (Ex 2.5): Dave and Les Jacobs/Blend Images; p. 78 (Ex 2.6): Devonyu/iStock/Getty Images Plus; p. 78 (Ex 2.7): adventtr/E+; p. 78 (Ex 2.8), p. 83 (TL): Grassetto/iStock/Getty Images Plus; p. 83 (CL): kvkirillov/iStock/Getty Images Plus; p. 83 (BL): ByoungJoo/iStock/Getty Images Plus; p. 83 (TC): Zoonar RF/Zoonar/Getty Images Plus; p. 83 (C): John Kasawa/iStock/Getty Images Plus; p. 83 (BC): ARTYuSTUDIO/iStock/Getty Images Plus; p. 83 (TR): f28production/iStock/Getty Images Plus; p. 83 (CR): RTimages/iStock/Getty Images Plus; p. 83 (BR): adventtr/iStock/Getty Images Plus; p. 84: Brent Winebrenner/Lonely Planet Images; p. 97 (Ex 3a): RobertoDavid/iStock/Getty Images Plus; p. 97 (Ex 3b): ollo/E+; p. 97 (Ex 3c): Marina Raith/Picture Press; p. 97 (Ex 3d): Rolf Bruderer/Blend Images; p. 97 (Ex 3e): Artur Azizkhanian/EyeEm; p. 97 (Ex 3f): Compassionate Eye Foundation/Chris Ryan/Taxi; p. 97 (Ex 3g): Tetra Images; p. 97 (Ex 3h): CasarsaGuru/iStock/Getty Images Plus; p. 99 (Ex 4a): Ariel Skelley/DigitalVision; p. 99 (Ex 4b): Tim Gerard Barker/Lonely Planet Images; p. 99 (Ex 4c): Hero Images; p. 99 (Ex 4d): Photo- Biotic/Photolibrary; p. 99 (Ex 4e): Dan Dunkley/Cultura; p. 99 (Ex 4f): Blend Images - JGI/Jamie Grill/Brand X Pictures; p. 101 (L): XiXinXing/iStock/Getty Images Plus; p. 101 (R): PhotoTalk/iStock/Getty Images Plus; p. 104 (L): monkeybusinessimages/iStock/Getty Images Plus; p. 104 (C): kadmy/iStock/Getty Images Plus; p. 104 (R): Bank215/iStock/Getty Images Plus; p. 106: Yuri_Arcurs/E+; p. 117 (Ex 3.1): lleerogers/E+; p. 117 (Ex 3.2): GeorgePeters/E+; p. 117 (Ex 3.3): Vichly44/ iStock/Getty Images Plus; p. 117 (Ex 3.4): DustyPixel/E+; p. 117 (3.5): Jasmina81/iStock/Getty Images Plus; p. 117 (Ex 3.6): ajafoto/iStock/Getty Images Plus; p. 121 (L): Jim Heimann Collection/Archive Photos; p. 121 (C): duckycards/E+; p. 121 (R): miflippo/iStock/Getty Images Plus.

**Illustrations**

p. 2, p. 13, p. 31, p. 38, p. 89, p. 113, p. 114: QBS Learning; p. 6, p. 33, p. 42, p. 66, p. 109: Mona Daly; p. 8 (Ex 2.1—2.6), p. 16, p. 37: Pamela Hobbs; p. 9: Frank Montagna; p. 11, p. 20, p. 32, p. 49, p. 54, p. 55, p. 70, p. 83, p. 102: Vilma Ortiz-Dillon; p. 18, p. 23, p. 30, p. 73, p. 75, p. 90, p. 125: John Batten; p. 20, p. 80: Ben Hasler; p. 47: Images Courtesy Precision Dynamics-St. John; p. 53, p. 85, p. 116: Peter Hoey.